Slap Bass Enc

by Josiah Garrett

This book is dedicated to all the teachers in my life. May it inspire you as they have inspired me.

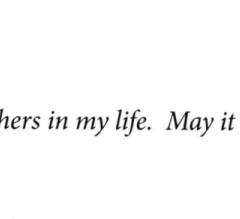

To access the online audio go to:
www.melbay.com/30657MEB

© 2018 by Mel Bay Publications, Inc. All Rights Reserved.
WWW.MELBAY.COM

TABLE OF CONTENTS

	Page	Audio
Key: Slap Style	4	
Key: Double Thump	5	
Key: Fretting Hand	6	
How to Practice	7	

ESSENTIAL PHRASES.......................... 8

	Page	Audio
Groups of 2	9	
Groups of 2 w/Double Thump	9	
Groups of 3	9	
Groups of 3 w/Double Thump	10	
Groups of 4	11	
Groups of 4 w/Double Thump	12	

READING THE EXERCISES.................. 14

SLAP STYLE...................................... 17

	Page	Audio
The Basics	18	
The Basics w/Mutes	18	1-32
Linear Slap Patterns	22	34-39
3-Muted Hit	25	40-46

DOUBLE THUMP............................... 27

	Page	Audio
The Basics	28	
The Basics w/Mutes	28	47-70
Linear: Double Thump Patterns	31	71-79
Muted Double Thump Down/Up Variations	36	80-93
3-Muted Hit	38	94-100

TABLE OF CONTENTS

	Page	Audio
PARADIDDLES	**41**	
Paradiddles: Slap	42	101-105
Paradiddles: Slap w/Mutes	43	106-112
Paradiddles: Double Thump	45	113-117
Paradiddles: Double Thump w/Mutes	46	118-121
TRIPLETS	**48**	
Triplets: Slap	49	122-131
Triplets: Slap w/Mutes	51	132-138
Triplets: Slap w/Hammer Option	53	139-140
Triplet-Ta: Slap	55	141-142
Triplet-Ta: Slap w/Mutes	56	143-149
Triplet-Ta: Slap w/Hammer Option	57	
Triplets: Double Thump	60	150
Triplets: Double Thump w/Mutes	61	151-156
Triplet-Ta: Double Thump	63	157-159
KHALIGI	**64**	
Khaligi: Slap	65	160-162
Khaligi: Slap w/Hammer Option	71	
Khaligi: Double Thump	73	163-165
Khaligi: Double Thump w/Hammer Option	77	
Khaligi: Double Thump w/Mutes	80	
EXTRA PHRASES	**83**	
Groups of 2 w/Mutes	84	
Groups of 3 w/Mutes	85	

KEY - GROUPS OF 1

SLAP STYLE

....

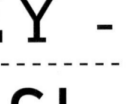

Thump

"Open a doorknob",
don't "Back-hand a tennis ball"

1. Shape your slapping hand into a "C" position.
2. Keep your pinky and ring finger rested against the body of your bass in a comfortable position.
3. Hold your thumb parallel to the strings, taut.
4. Pivot your slapping hand around the axis created by your index finger and upper forearm.
5. By applying rotational force around that axis, "thump" the string with a quick strike; release.
6. Imagine your thumb like a drumstick bouncing off of the head of a snare drum.

....

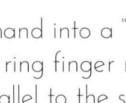

Pop

"Pull a trigger",
don't "Throw a frisbee"

1. Shape your slapping hand into a "C" position.
2. While keeping your ring and pinky fingers of your slapping hand touching the body of the bass, pluck the string outward and away from the body.
3. Hold your thumb parallel to the strings, taut.
4. Engage your fingers like hooks to pluck and then "pop" off of each string.
5. Practice popping with both your index and middle fingers on similar and alternating strings.

....

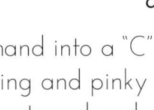

Muted Note

1. With your fretting hand, place your fingers over the strings so that no audible pitch is made upon the note being struck.
2. With your fretting hand, use delicate and firm fingers to keep muted hits quick and clean.
3. Do not let the Muted Note resonate.

**Imagine a Muted Note having the same timbre quality as a closed Hi-Hat or rim shot on a snare.

KEY - GROUPS OF 1 DOUBLE THUMP

Double Thump Down

"Give a handshake", don't "Have a thumb-war"

1. Hold your slapping hand in a "C" position.
2. Keep your pinky and ring finger rested against the body of your bass in a comfortable position.
3. While keeping your thumb taught, engage your whole hand/forearm in the double thump-down motion.
4. In one fluid movement, push your thumb "through" the string and rest it on the string below.
5. Allow the string you've just thumped to resonate cleanly.

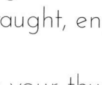

Double Thump Up

1. Hold your slapping hand in a "C" position
2. Keep your pinky and ring finger rested against the body of your bass in a comfortable position.
3. While keeping your thumb taught, engage your whole hand/forearm in the double thump-up motion.
4. In one fluid movement, pull your thumb "through" the string and briefly suspend it in the air above the string.
5. Allow the string you've just thumped to resonate cleanly.

Double Thump Up (In Parentheses)

1. Implies that if the exercise is being repeated: the first note should be struck as double thump-up.
2. If the exercise is not being repeated: the first note should be struck as a normal "Thump".
**This symbol only appears when a double thump-down is the final hit of the exercise.

KEY - GROUPS OF 1

FRETTING HAND

Hammer-On/ Hammer Option

1. With your fretting hand, strike a fret with precision and force.
2. Allow the note you've just struck to resonate cleanly.
3. Be aware of the dynamics when performing a Hammer-On
*Hammer Option: If singular, you have the option of a Hammer-On or a Hammer-Off.

Hammer-Off (Pull-Off)

1. With your fretting hand, release a previously struck note.
2. Pull down/push up on the string with your fretting hand so the string resonates after your fretting finger is removed.
3. Allow the note you've just released to resonate cleanly.
4. Be aware of the dynamics when performing a Hammer-Off.
**This symbol only appears in a phrase that also includes a Hammer-On or Palm Mute/Hammer Option.

Palm Mute

1. With your fretting hand, strike the string in a percussive manner so that no audible pitch is heard when striking the string.
2. Perform the Palm Mute similarly to a Hammer-On, but do not let the string resonate.

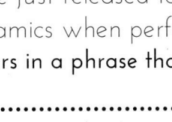

Palm Mute/ Hammer Option

1. This symbol indicates a place where a Palm Mute and a Hammer Option are interchangeable.

HOW TO PRACTICE

The Slap Bass Encyclopedia is a rhythmic theory book for slap bass. Inspiration for these exercises is derived from the massive collections of snare rudiments and rhythms shared by teachers around the world. These exercises are designed to improve your technical abilities, precision and timing, rhythmic awareness, speed and accuracy, endurance, versatility, and dexterity. Adhere to the guidelines below in order for a more efficient use of practice time, thorough understanding of the content, and comprehensive slap bass technique.

For your speed, accuracy, and precision:

Practicing too fast is the most detrimental way to develop the skills that enable you to play with speed, accuracy, and precision. When you practice at a fast BPM, you are unable to identify the subtle mistakes in your technique and performance. The key to incorporating these phrases into your play-style with speed, accuracy, and precision is to practice them as slowly as you need to execute them cleanly and correctly.

- Establish a BPM value as your starting tempo when practicing new content.
- As you progress through the book and become more comfortable with these phrases and your ability to perform them, begin to raise the BPM.
- Consider a clean, precise performance at a comfortable and "musical" BPM as a reflection of a high level of competency for that phrase or group.
- Once you feel comfortable with these Phrases, practice first alternating strings, then move on to practicing these phrases through scales, modes, chord progressions, grooves, and melodies.
- Experiment by adding different groups of 2, 3, and 4 together to create unique extended slap patterns!

For your dexterity, versatility, and endurance:

Slap Bass is a highly physical technique. Endurance training improves your muscle memory and dexterity as a slap bass player, including knowledge of the physiology of your arms and hands and how to take care of them.

- Maintain a calm, steady breath while practicing.
- Before you play = Cardio! I recommend 5 minutes.
  After you play = Stretch! I recommend 10 minutes.
- Apply ice as needed to tense or inflamed muscles and tendons after your practice (not before!).
- Apply heat as needed for more efficient stretching and to improve blood flow to muscles and tendons.
- Do not force your arms or fingers! "Dance" with them across the strings.
- Slap Bass is all about Muscle Memory!
- Don't be afraid to take breaks!

As a general rule when practicing these exercises: **Fast is Last!**

For the best results, practice for 15 minutes a day, every day.

A WORD OF CAUTION:

If you feel your forearms, elbow, wrist, hands or fingers tense up while practicing, pause to rest.

If you ever feel pain in those areas, STOP playing! Apply Ice + Heat as soon as possible!

If this continues to occur, you may be practicing the exercises too fast. Rest your arms, and slow down your practice to a more reasonable tempo.

About This Section

"If you can execute each individual type of slap technique, then hypothetically you can perform every grouping of 2 hits. If you can execute every group of 2 and also each individual hit, then hypothetically you can perform every group of 3. If you can execute every group of 2, 3 and each individual hit, then hypothetically you can perform every group of 4. From there, any assortment of slap patterns for any duration is possible."

These essential phrases are the building blocks for your slap bass technique. **This is the philosophy behind Slap Bass Encyclopedia.**

*The "Groups of 2" and "Groups of 3" are accompanied by their muted possibilities at the end of this book in addition to the non-muted groupings. The "Groups of 4" are not accompanied by muted possibilities simply because there are so many of them.

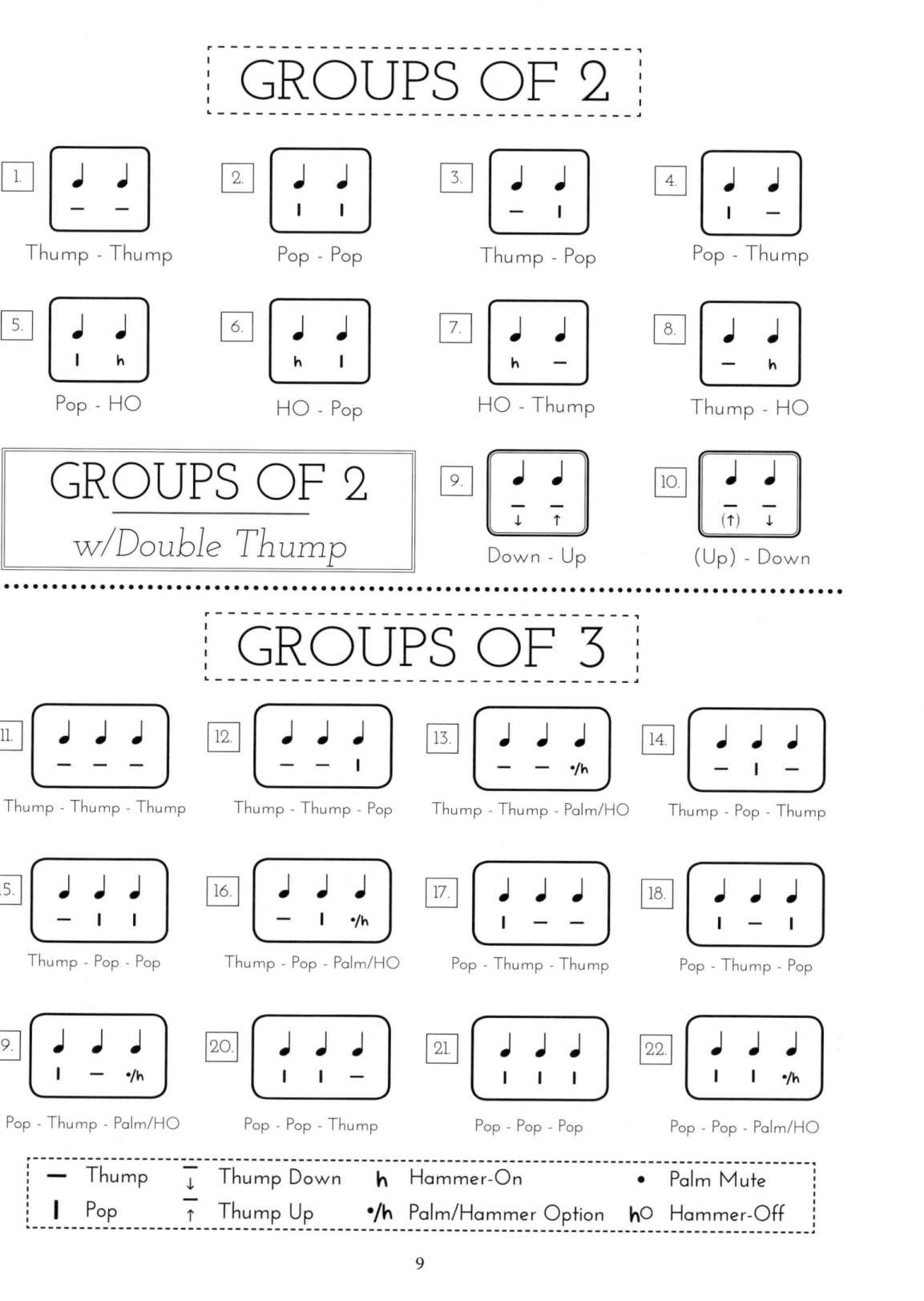

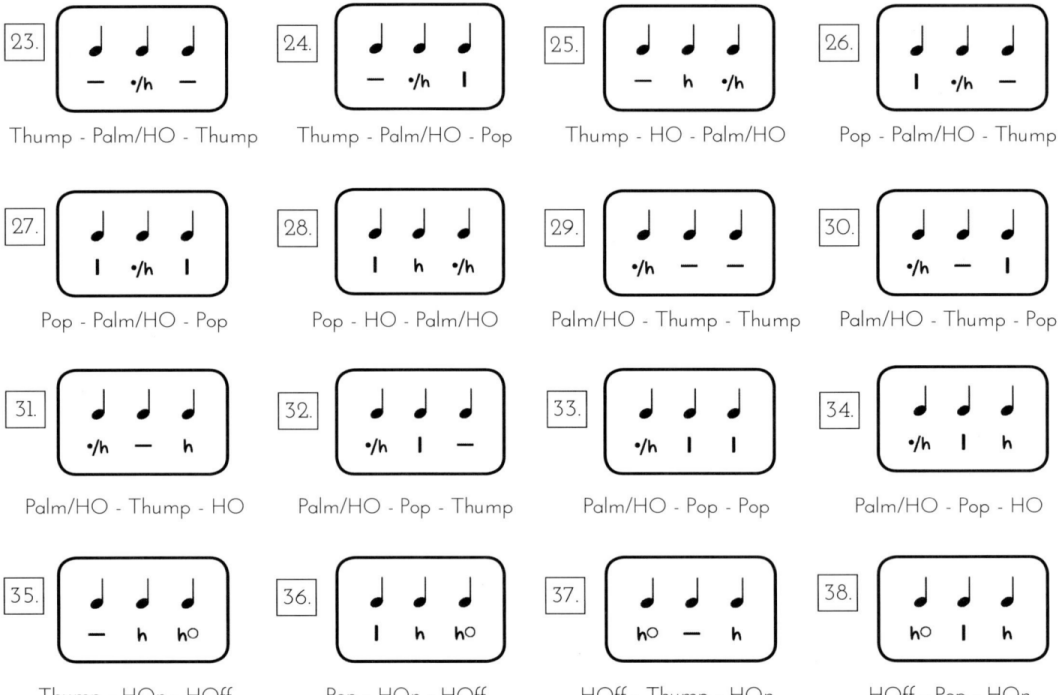

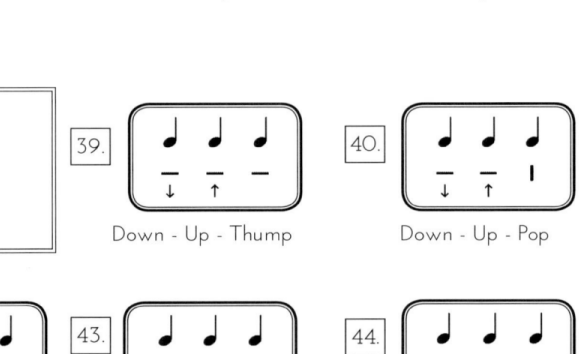

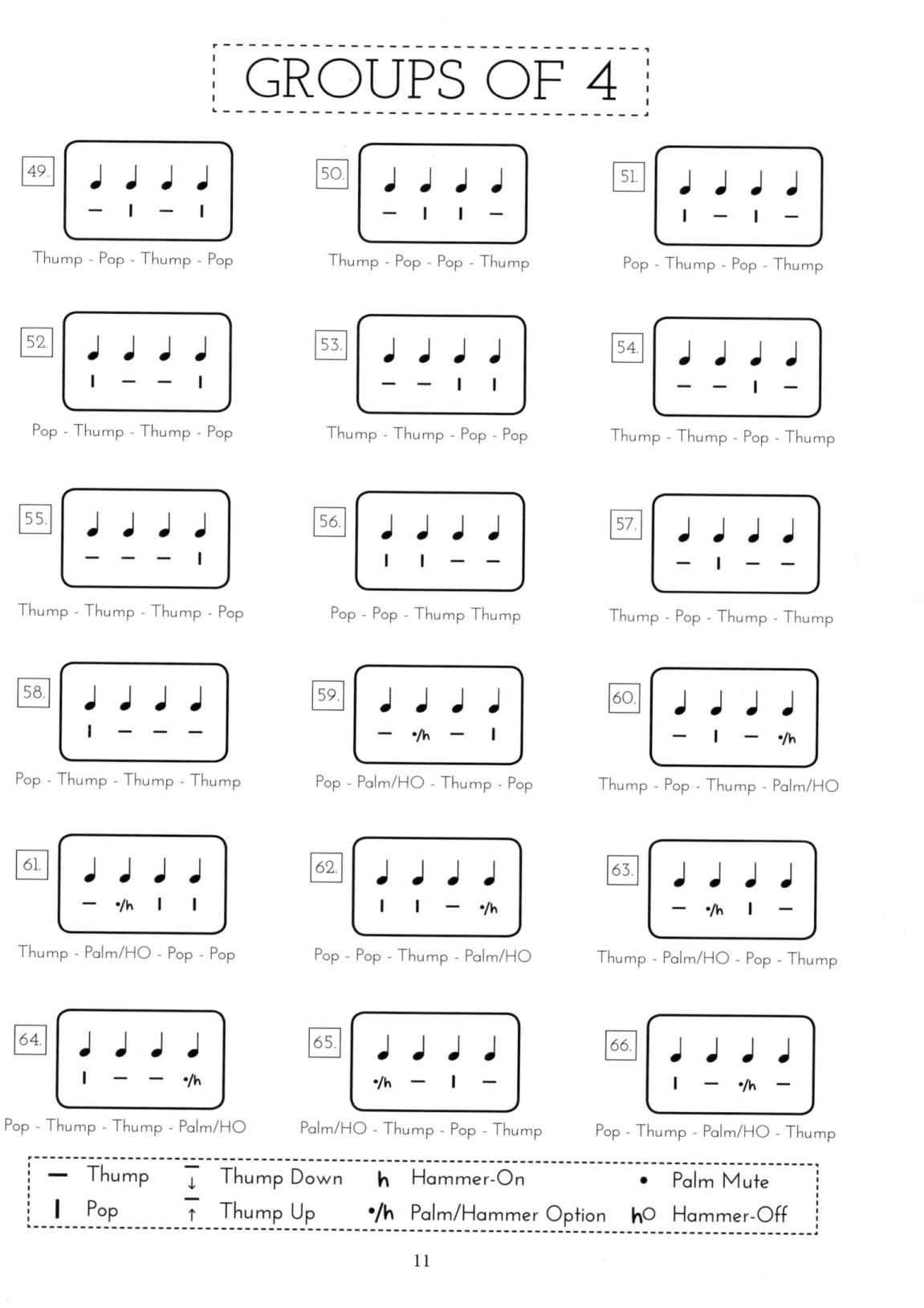

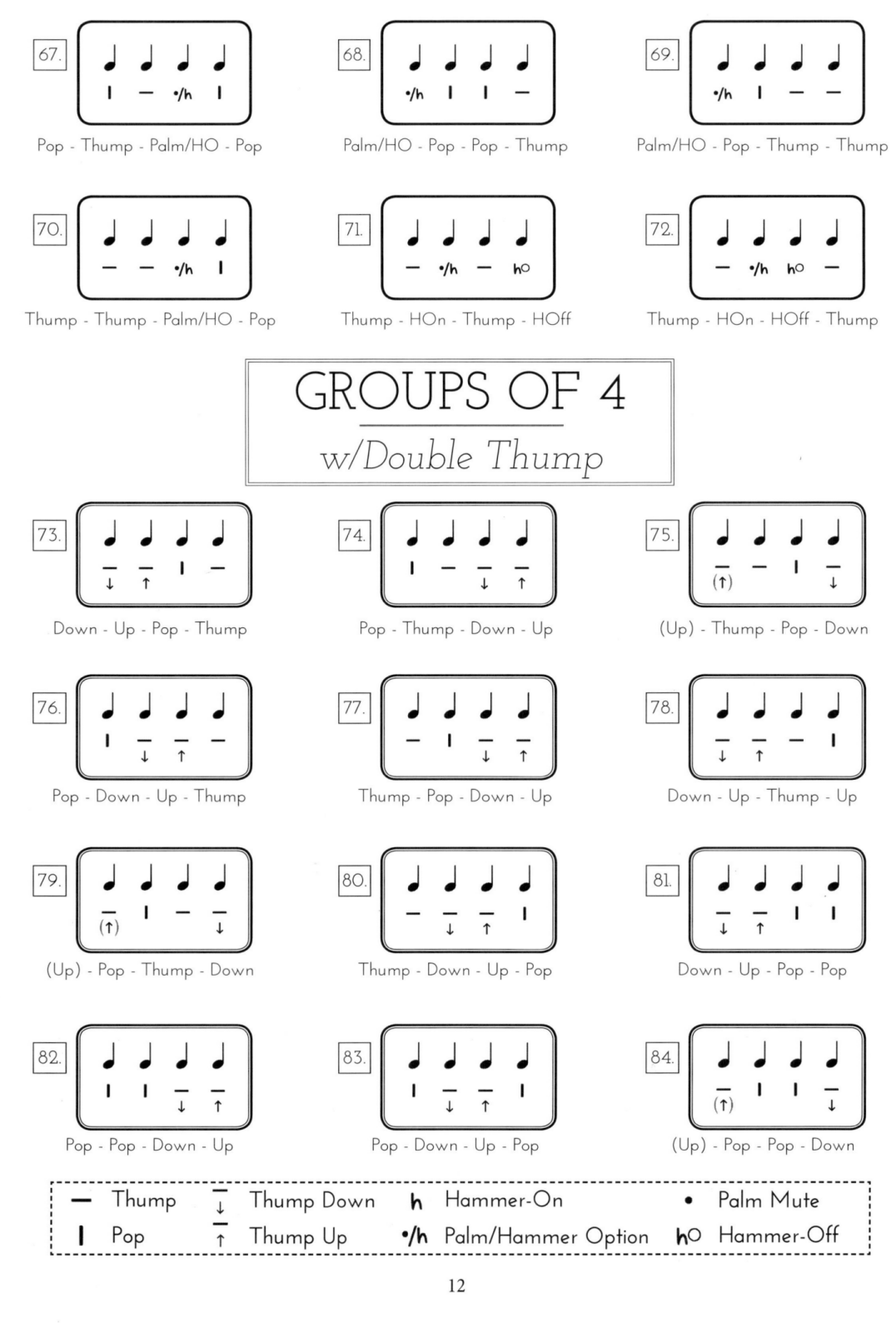

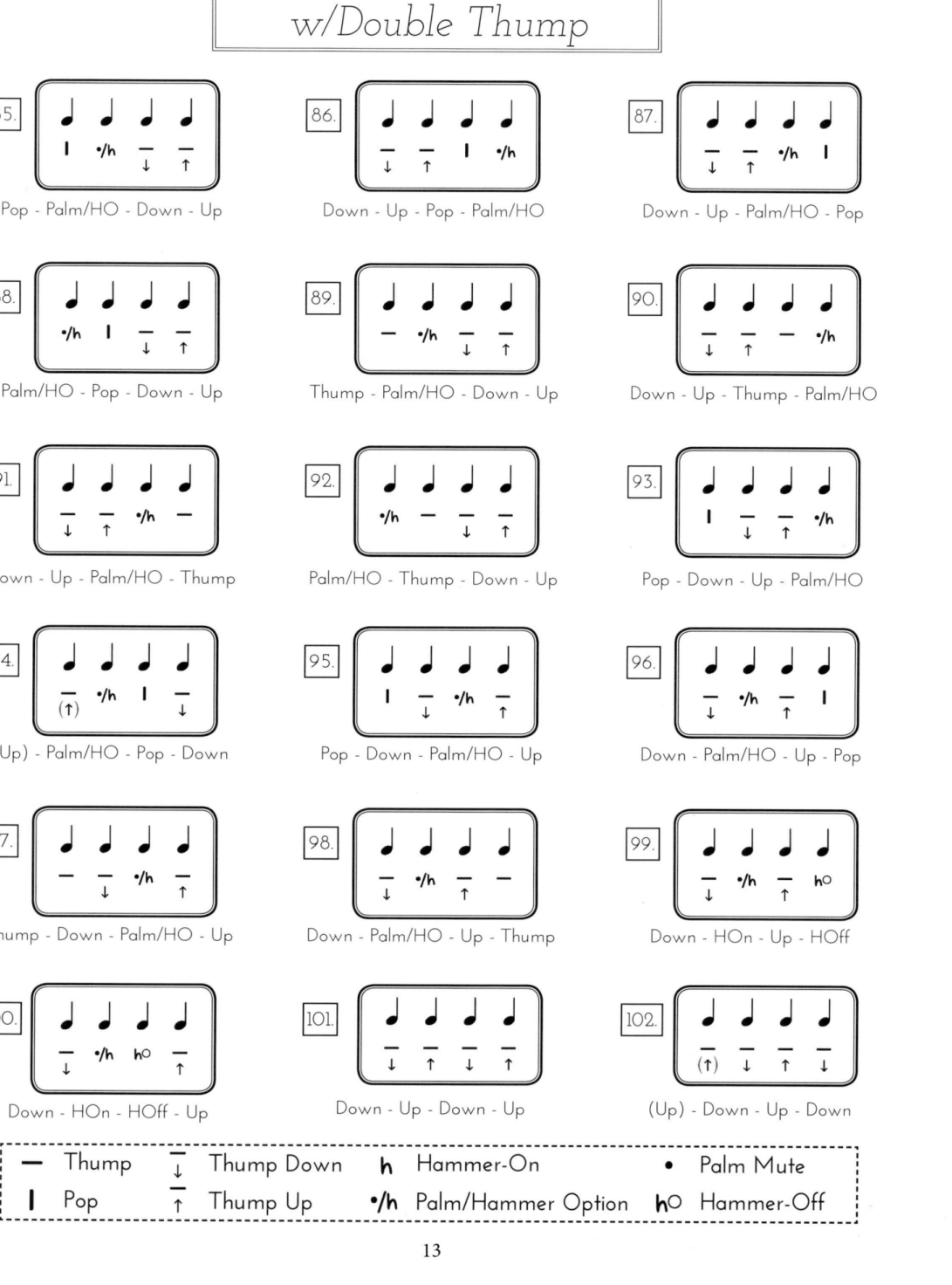

READING THE EXERCISES

Exercises in this book are divided into sets of 2, 3, and 4. Exercises in sets of 2 are organized differently than sets of 3, which are different than sets of 4. Each set of exercises is dependent on the content it is comprised of. These next 3 pages detail the organizational methods for the exercises throughout the rest of the book.

EXERCISES IN SETS OF 2

INVERSION
The second exercise is the inverse of the first.

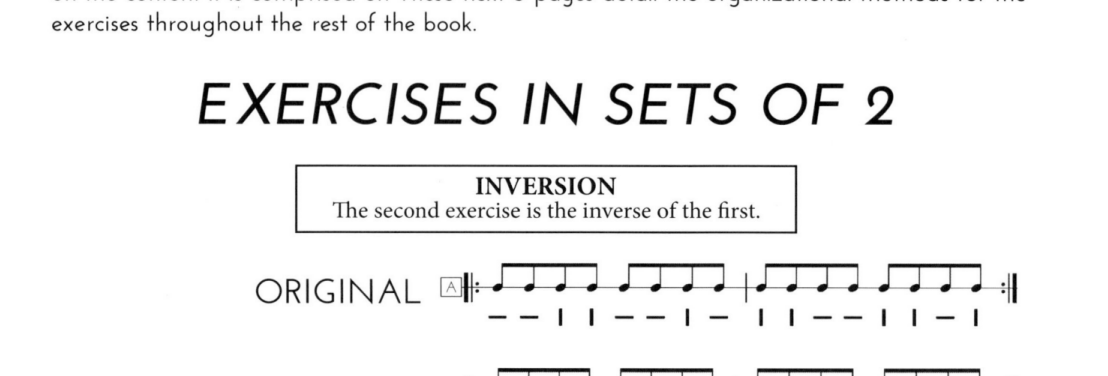

STRONG BEAT/WEAK BEAT
The first exercise places emphasis on the Strong Beat while the second places emphasis on the Weak Beat.

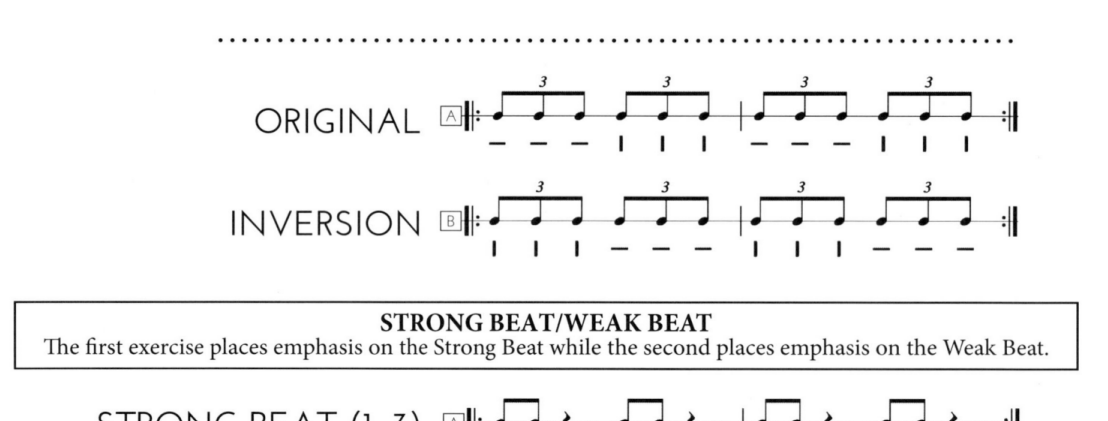

EXERCISES IN SETS OF 3

TRIPLETS

The original exercise is a Triplet. The 1st variation shifts the rhythm by one beat, placing the downbeat of the rhythm as the 3rd note of the Triplet. The 2nd Variations places the downbeat as the 2nd note of the Triplet.

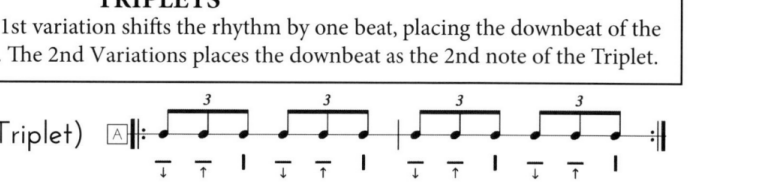

MUTED TRIPLETS

The original exercise is a Triplet with muted note(s). The first variation places the muted note(s) in the 2nd possible position within the Triplet. The 2nd variation places the muted note(s) in their 3rd possible position.

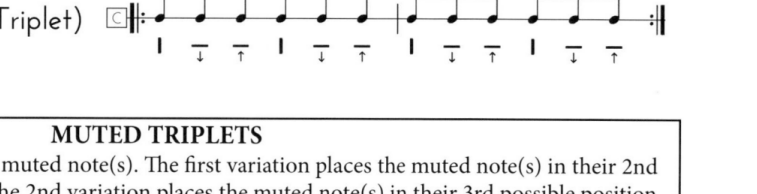

KHALIGI

The first exercise will follow a rhythmic pattern of 3-3-2. The second exercise will follow a rhythmic pattern of 3-2-3. The third exercise will follow a pattern of 2-3-3.

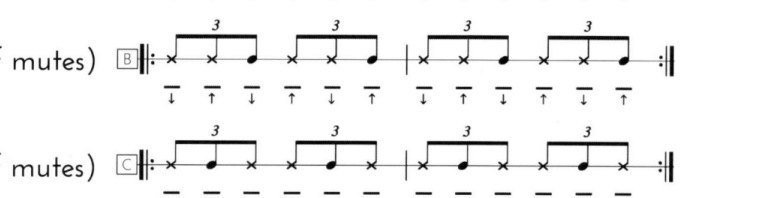

EXERCISES IN SETS OF 4

4/4 RHYTHMS

The first exercise places emphasis on the Strong Beat. The second exercise places emphasis on the Weak Beat. The third exercise places emphasis on the AND of 1, known as Strong Beat Syncopation. The fourth exercise places emphasis on the AND of 2, known as Weak Beat Syncopation.

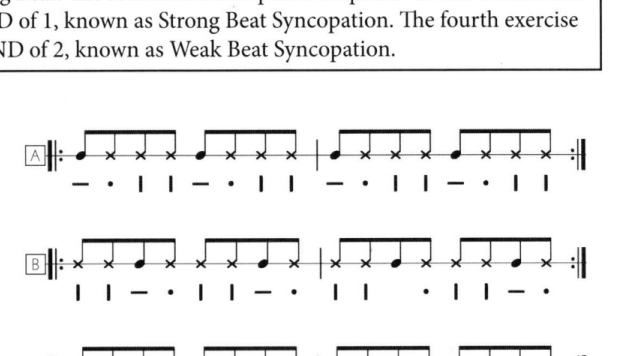

3/4 RHYTHMS

The first exercise is the original Triplet. The second is the Inverse of the first. The third is the a combination of ½ Original and ½ Inversion. The fourth is a combination of ½ Original and ½ Inversion in the opposite fashion.

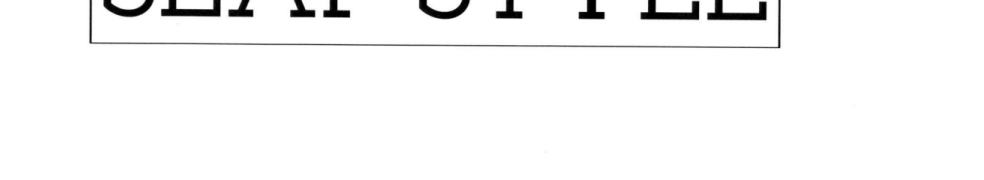

About This Section

These exercises focus on Slap and Thump strikes, as well as palm mutes and muted slaps and thumps.

These rhythms are best suited for chord progression, grooves, and melodies, as well as scales moving horizontally up and down the neck.

When practicing these rhythms, emphasize clean strikes for sustained string resonance. These rhythms are designed to confront and test your rhythmic awareness within a slap bass groove, thus it is more beneficial to perform each one slowly rather than a couple of your favorites at very fast speeds.

New calloused locations will form on the sides of your popping fingers and thumb.

*Stop practicing these if you feel pain or irritation from the repeated (and often intense) skin-to-string contact. These callouses will form, but it takes repeated practice and time to do so.

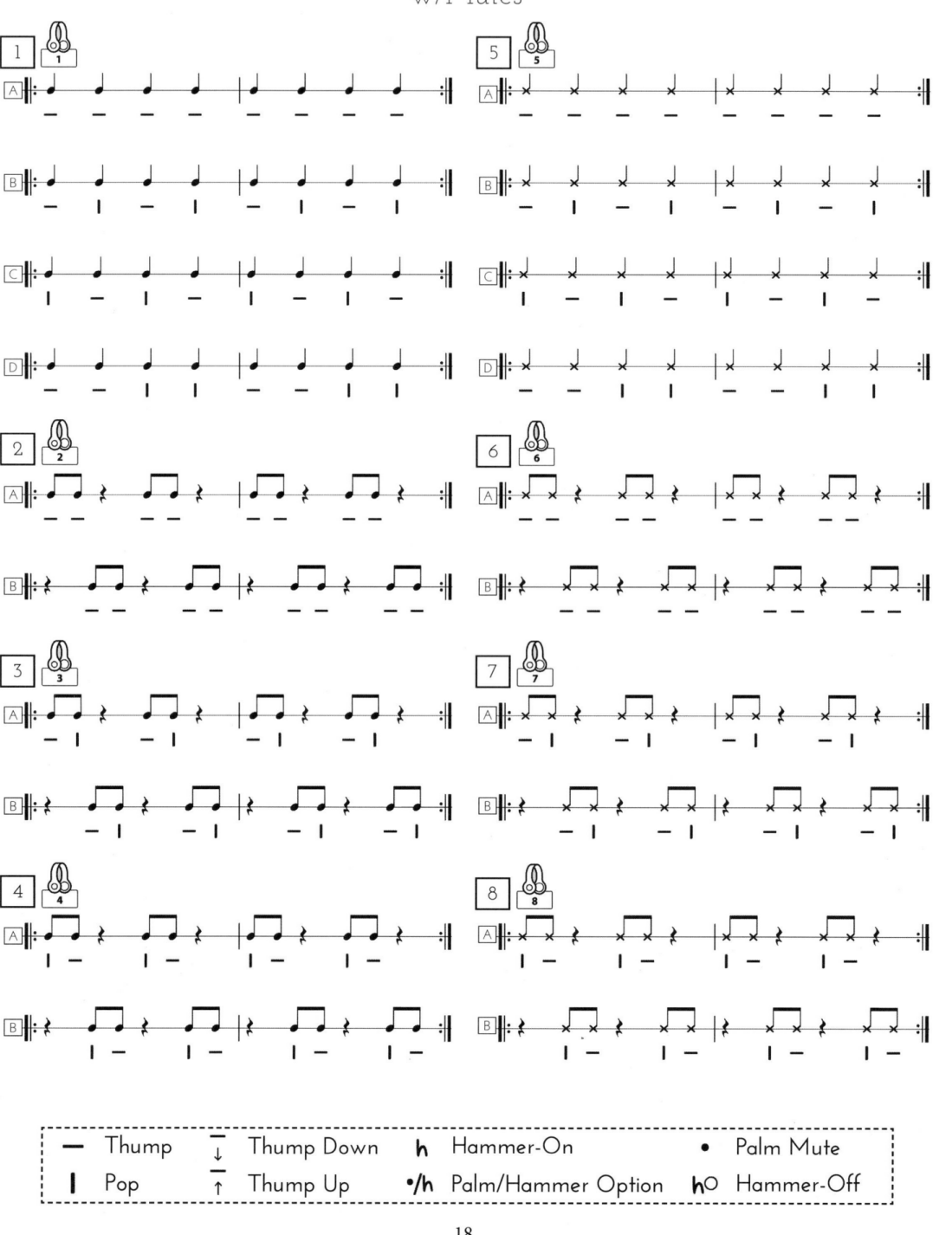

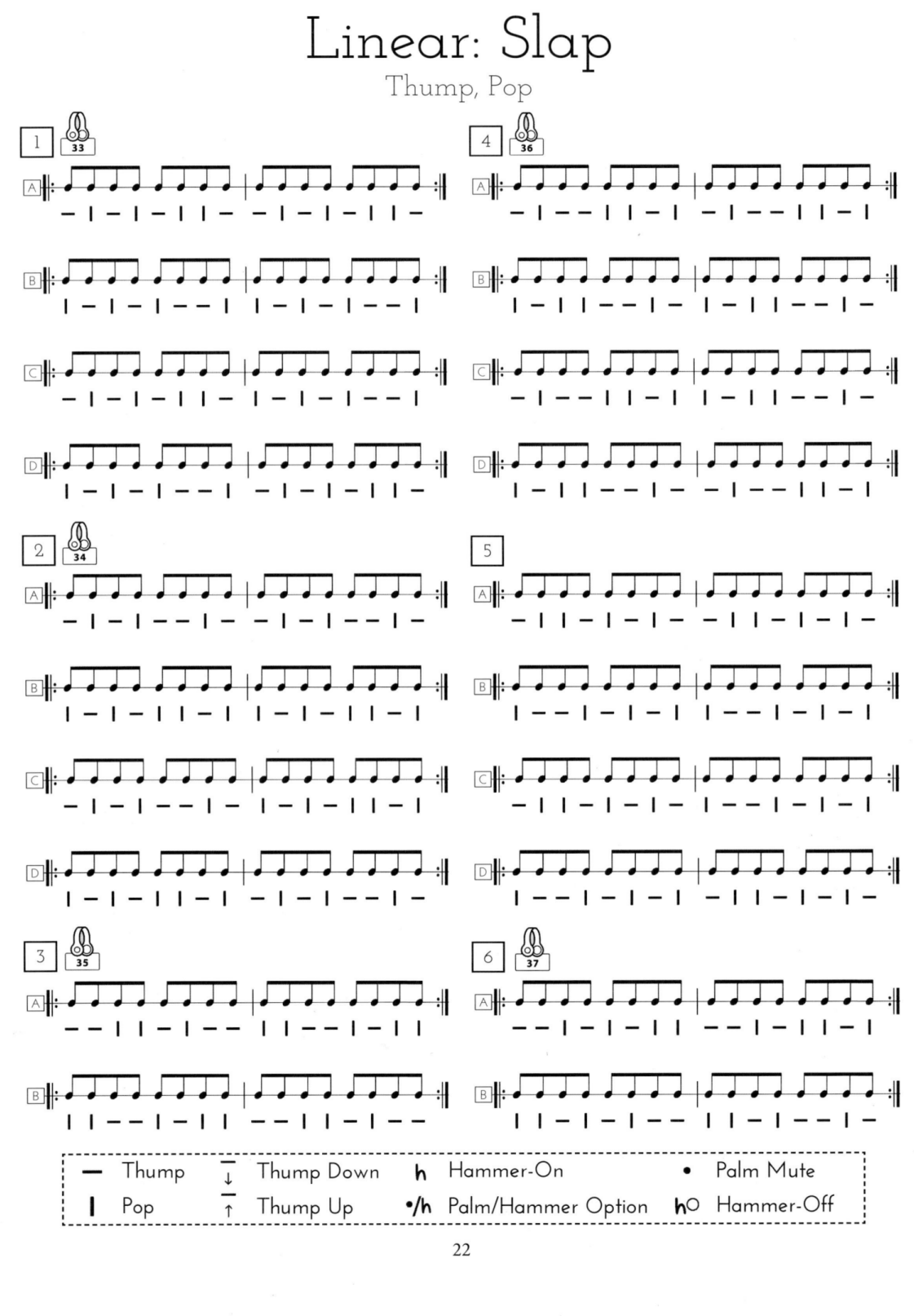

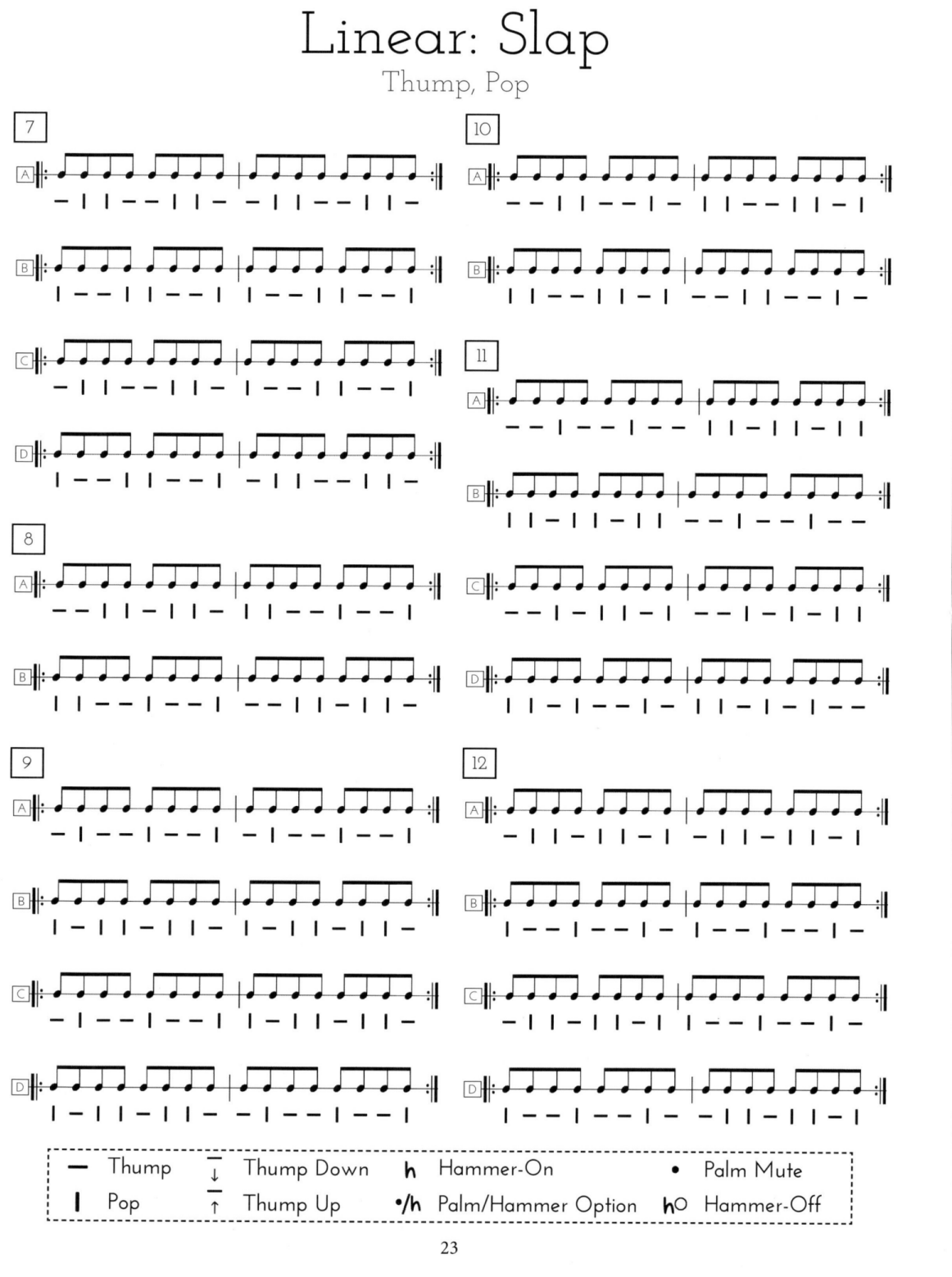

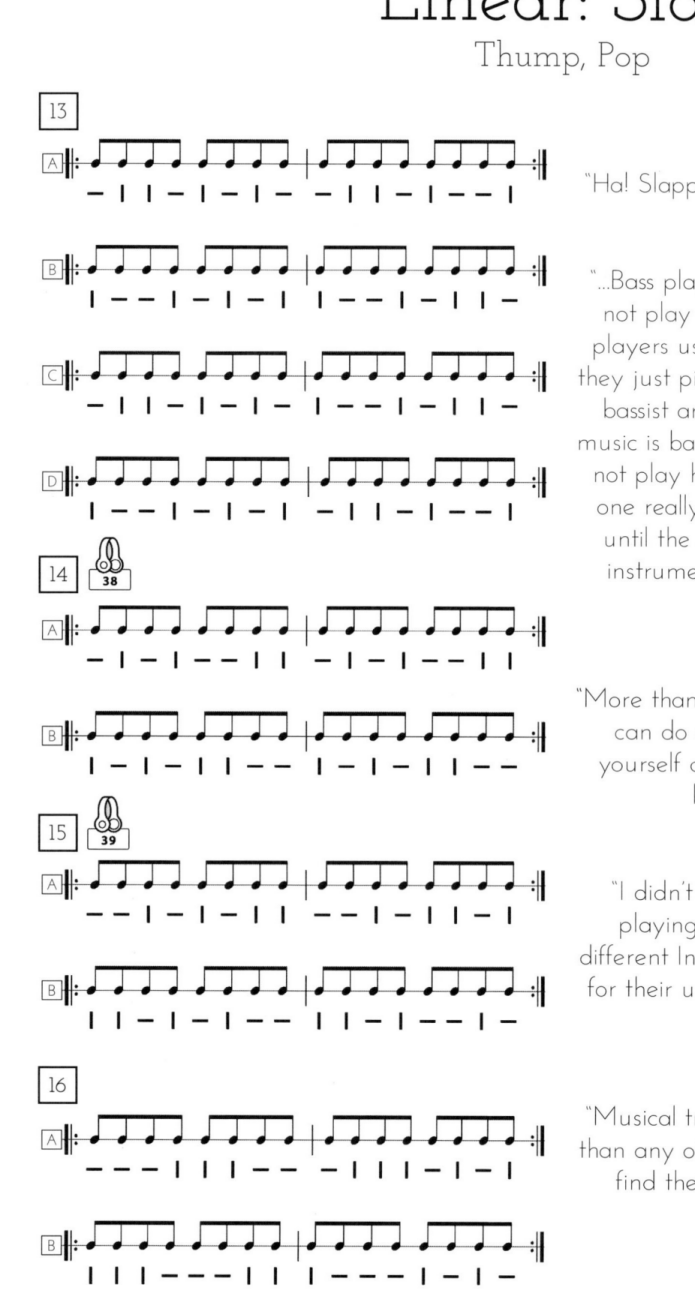

"Ha! Slapping, the ketchup of the bass world!"
- *Anthony Jackson*

"...Bass players at the beginning of jazz could not play their instrument. Most of the bass players used to be ex-trombone players and they just picked the bass because there was no bassist around. So the whole basis for jazz music is based on the fact that the bassist could not play his instrument. Isn't that funny? No one really realized it and really addressed it until the bass players who could play their instrument came along and started doing something with it."
- *Miroslav Vitous*

"More than anything, I think the best thing you can do as an artist is just stay as true to yourself as possible and hope that your fan base will appreciate that."
- *Les Claypool*

"I didn't follow the standard rules of bass playing, and many musicians on many different Instruments who became noteworthy for their unique or particular style did a very similar thing."
- *Billy Sheehan*

"Musical training is a more potent instrument than any other, because rhythm and harmony find their way into the inward places of the soul."
- *Plato*

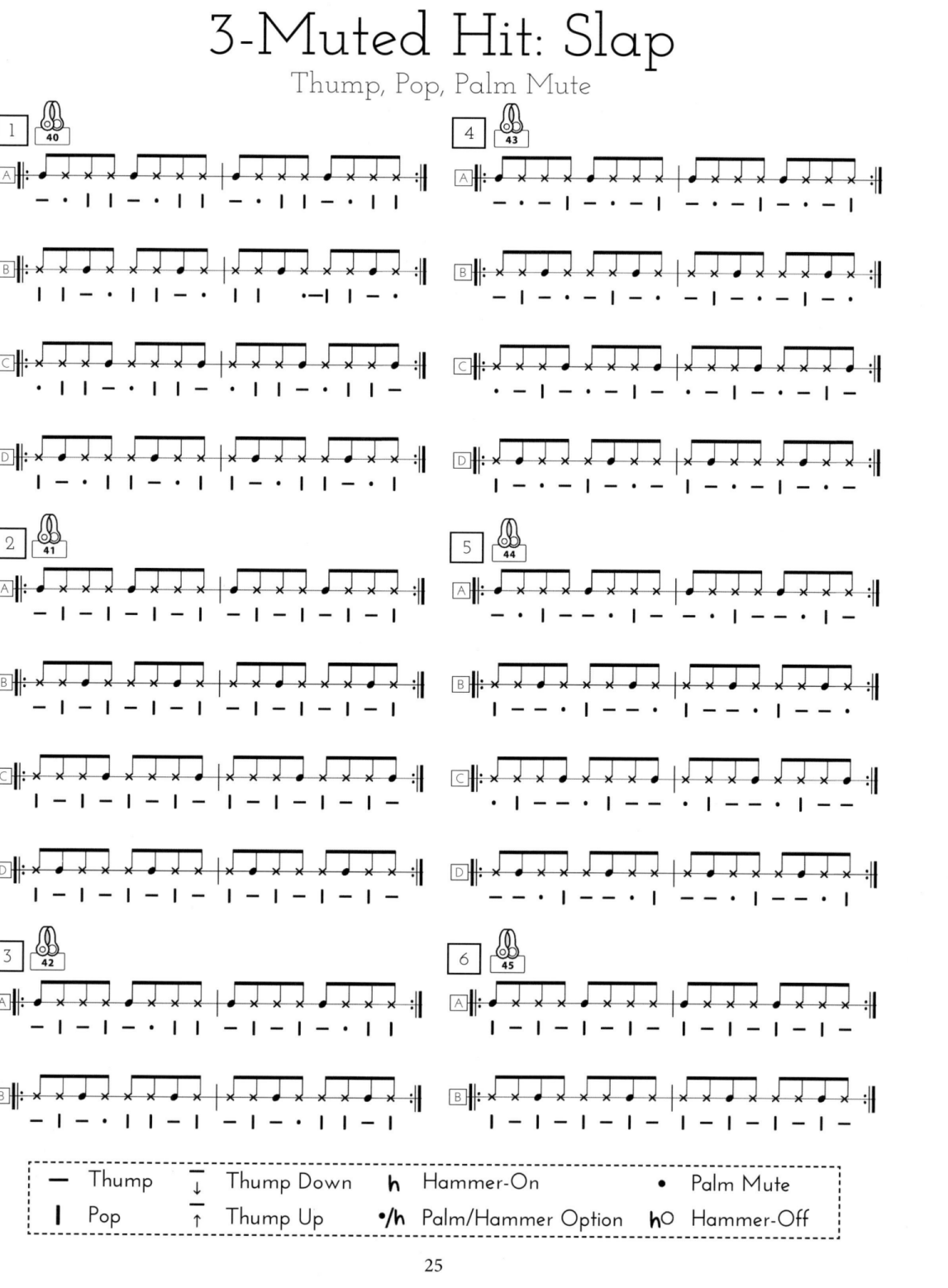

3-Muted Hit: Slap

Thump, Pop, Palm Mute

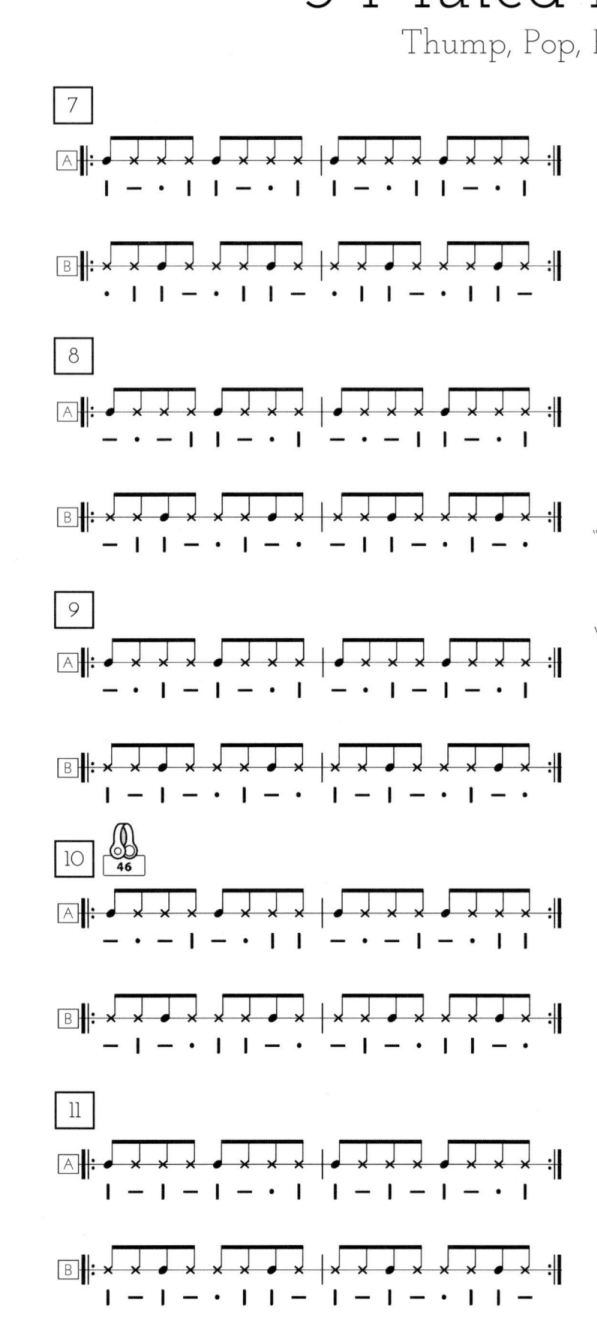

"I wouldn't want to hear Beethoven without beautiful bass, the cellos, the tuba. It's very important. Hip-hop has thunderous bass. And so does Beethoven. If you don't have the bass, it's like being amputated. It's like you have no legs."
- ***Lou Reed***

"Bass players are always the intellectual kind, but nobody knows it."
- ***Stanley Clarke***

"The bass, no matter what kind of music you're playing, it just enhances the sound and makes everything sound more beautiful and full. When the bass stops, the bottom kind of drops out of everything."
- ***Charlie Haden***

"Black Sabbath was written on bass: I just walked into the studio and went, bah, bah, bah, and everybody joined in and we just did it."
- ***Geezer Butler***

"I wonder if I could make an electric bass."
- ***Leo Fender***

"The bass player's function, along with the drums, is to be the engine that drives the car... everything else is merely colors."
- ***Suzi Quatro***

"It's not the notes you play, it's the notes you don't play."
-***Miles Davis***

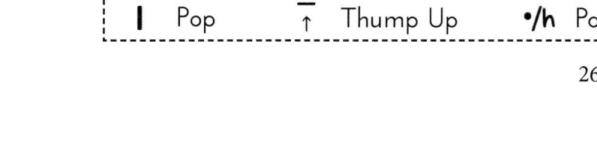

DOUBLE THUMP

About This Section

These rhythms use Double Thump technique, in addition to Thump, Pop, and Hammer-On and Hammer-Offs. These rhythms can be practiced through vertical scales and melodies with more success that the slap style exercises.

When practicing Double Thump, make sure to emphasize clean thumps that result in sustained resonance on the thumped string.

*When practicing up-thumb strokes for the first time, avoid striking the string with the edge of your thumbnail or you will damage the skin around the thumbnail. Try to strike the string with the fatty edge of your thumb on both the up and down thumb strokes. Eventually, the nerve endings in your thumb will harden just as they have on your finger tips, but it takes time. This is a unique place to build callouses, so stop practicing double thump if the skin around your thumb becomes red or if you ever feel pain from repeated contact with the string.

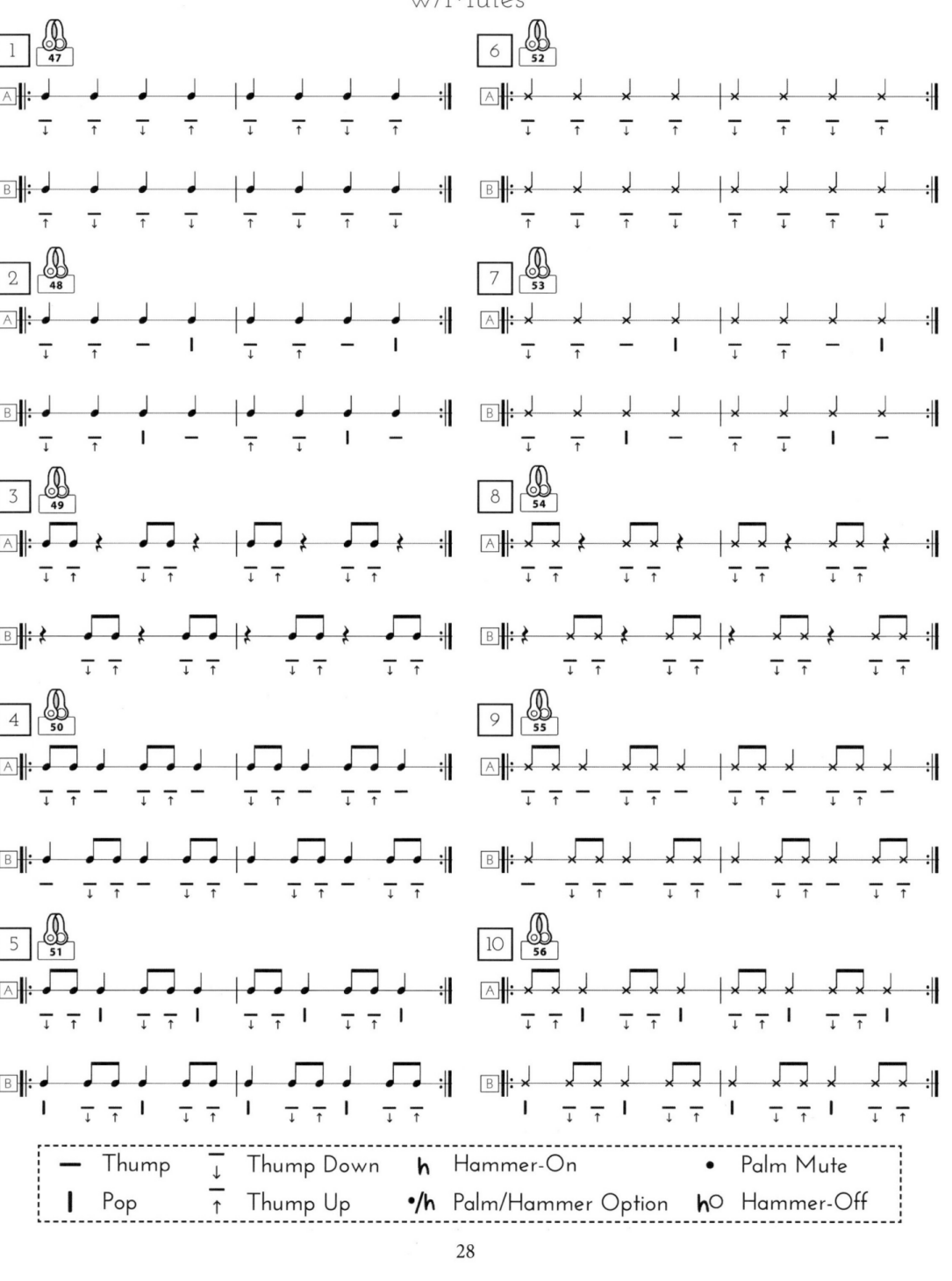

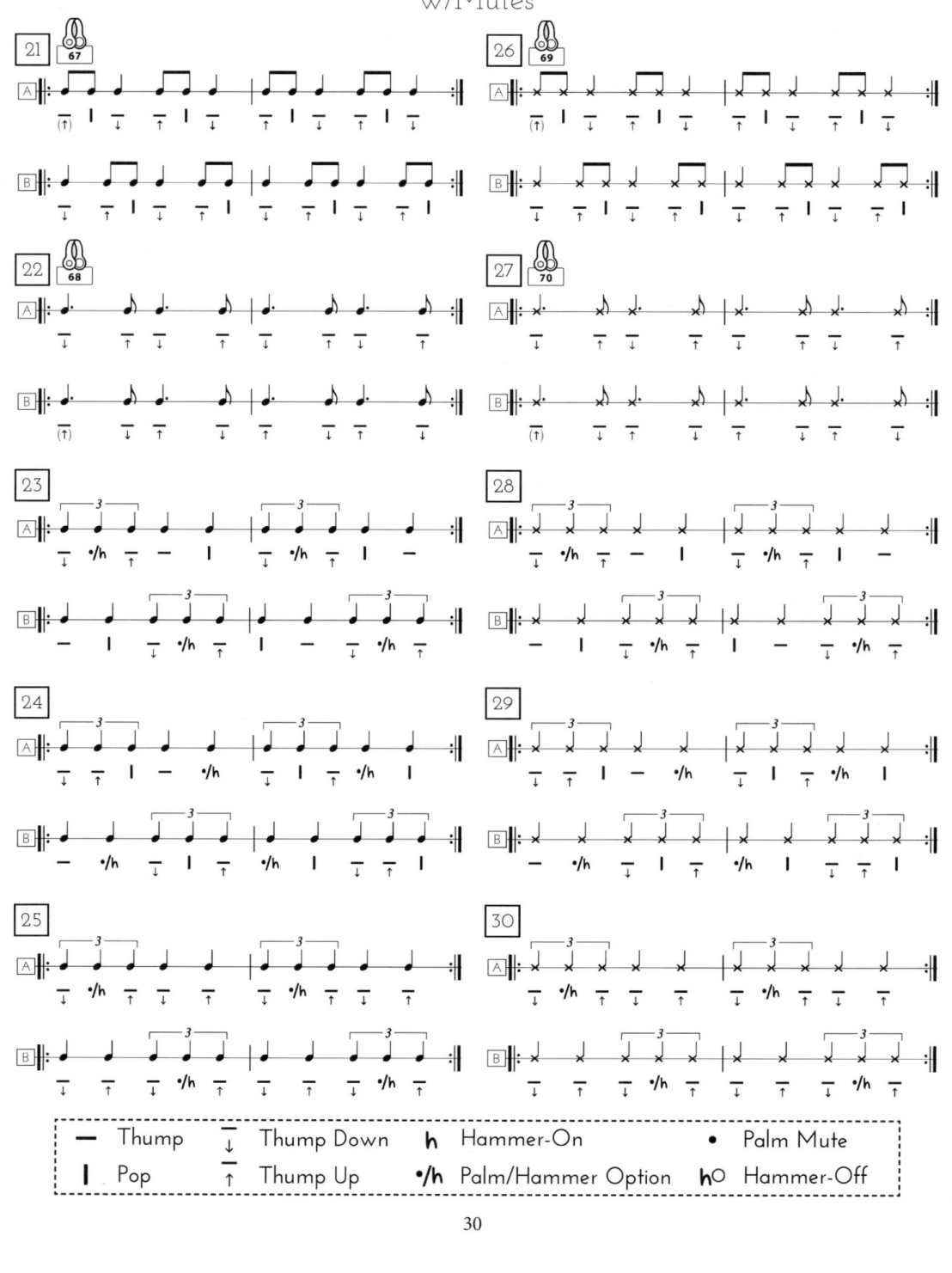

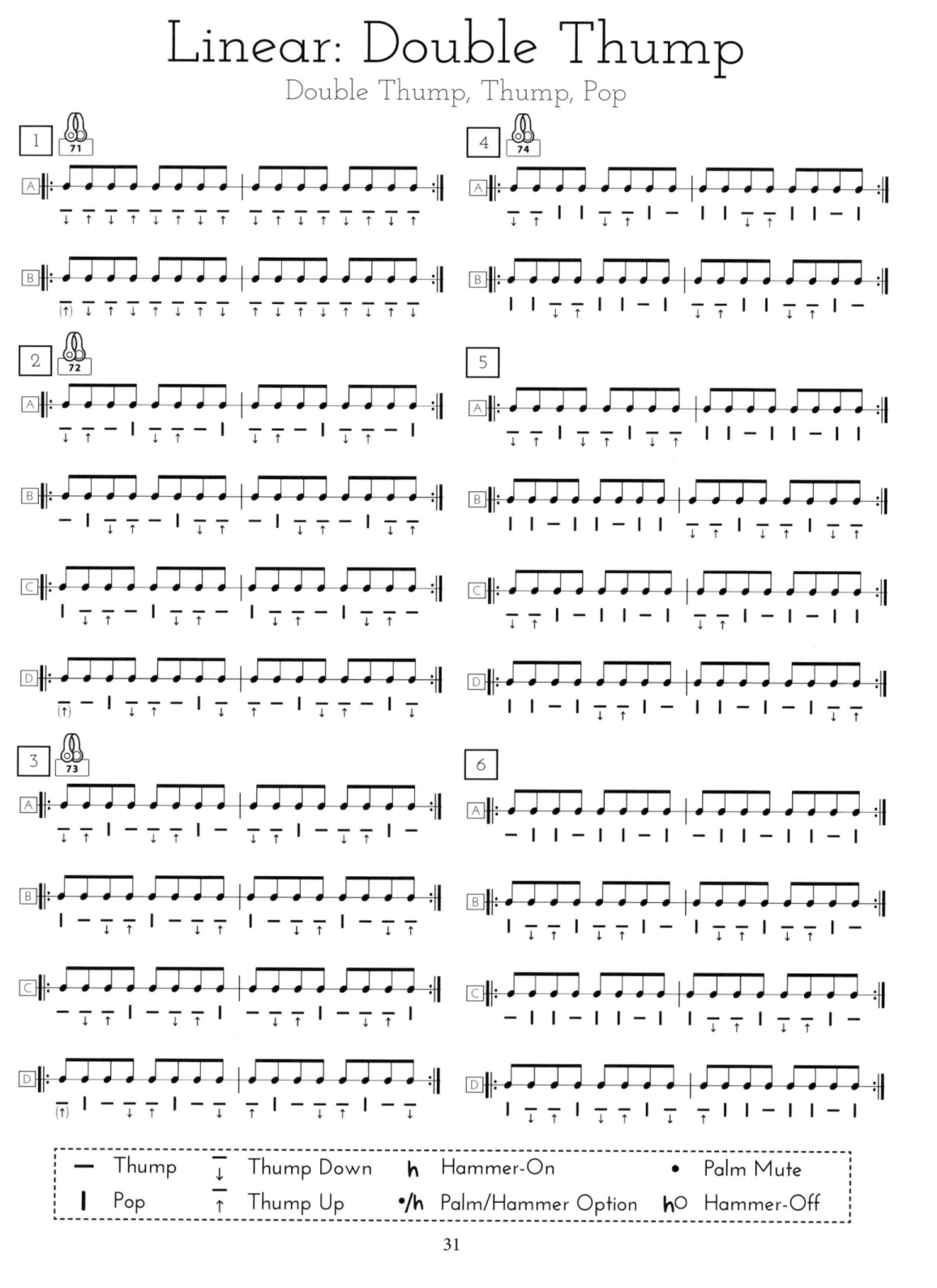

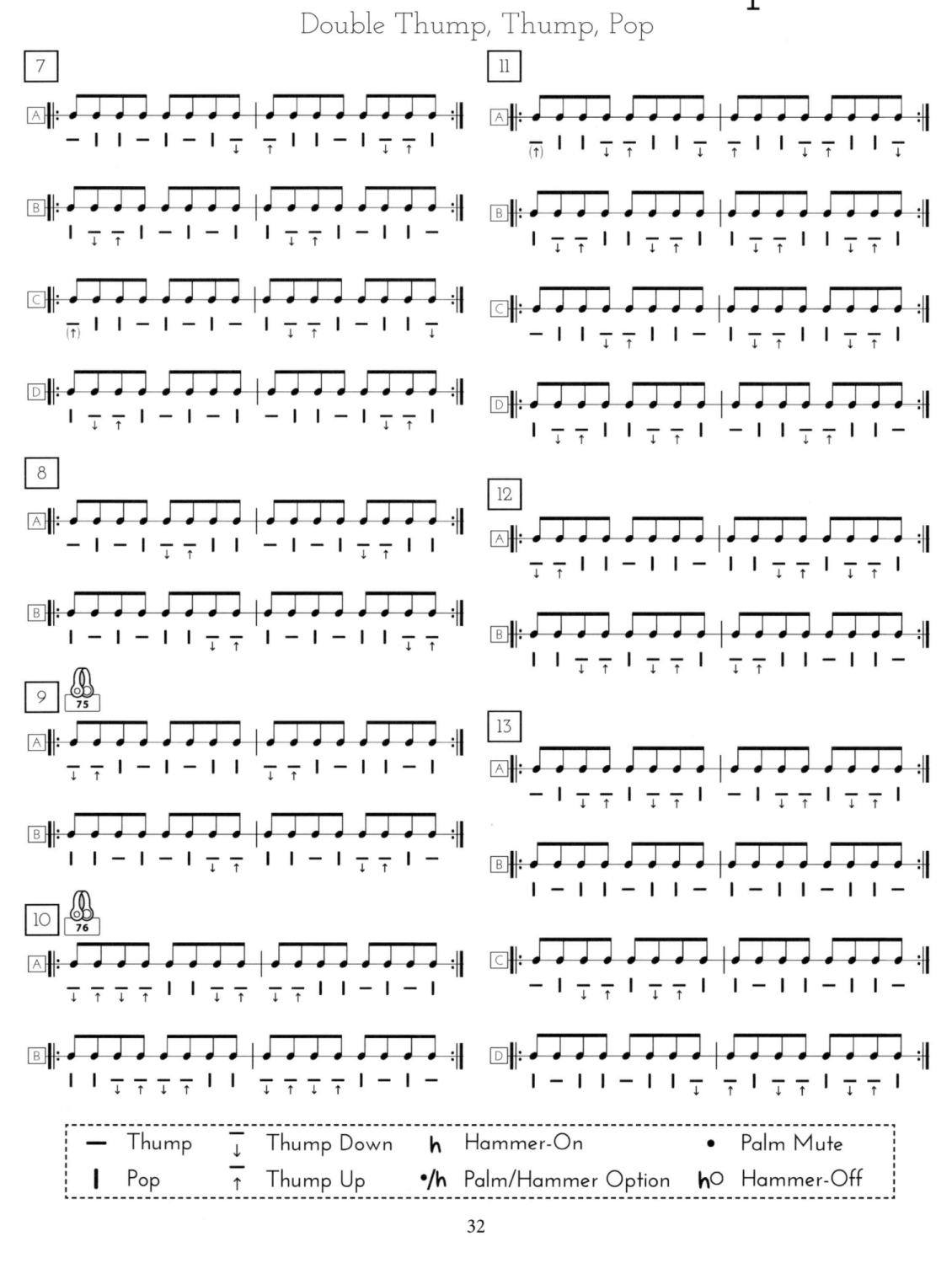

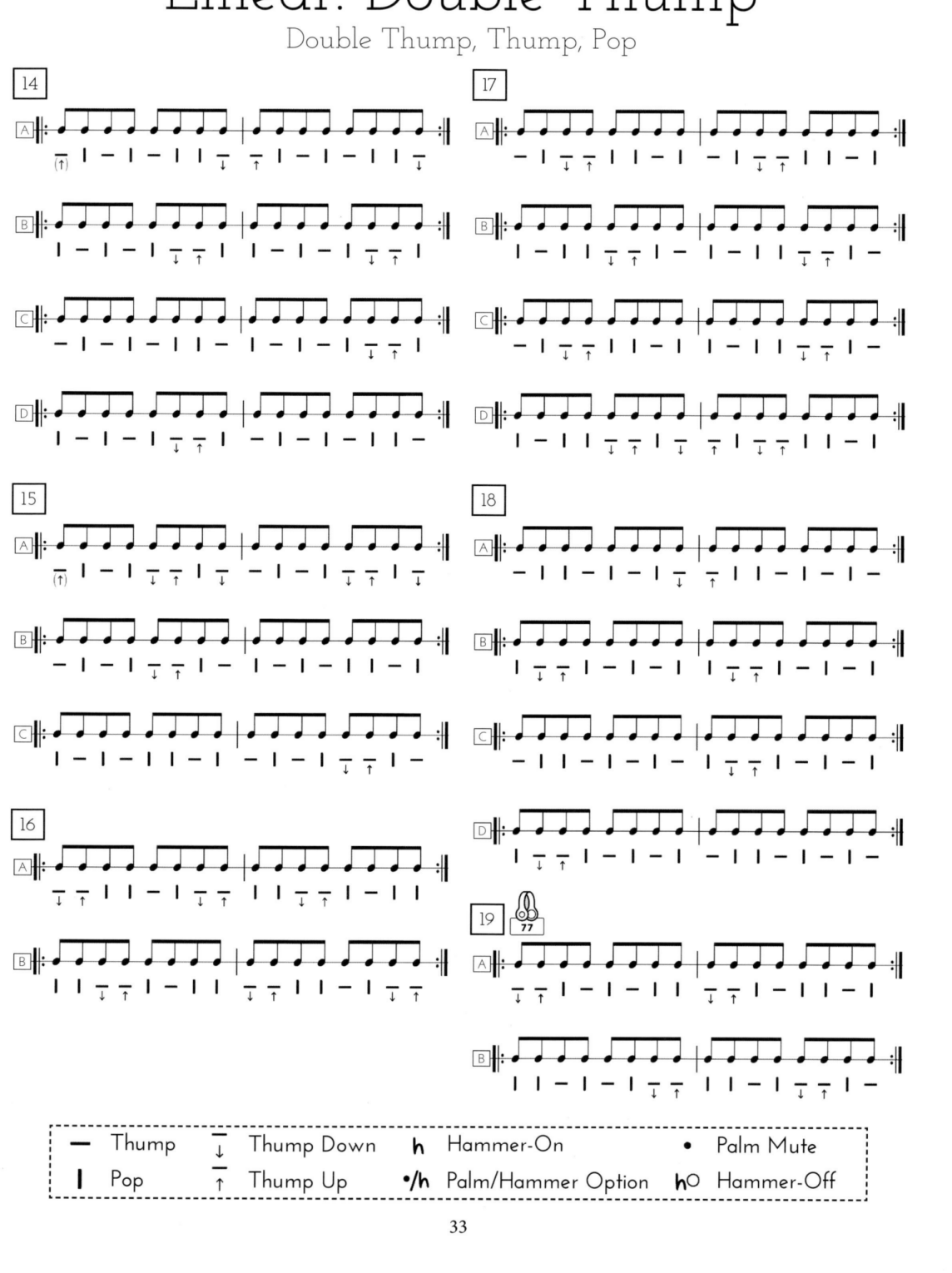

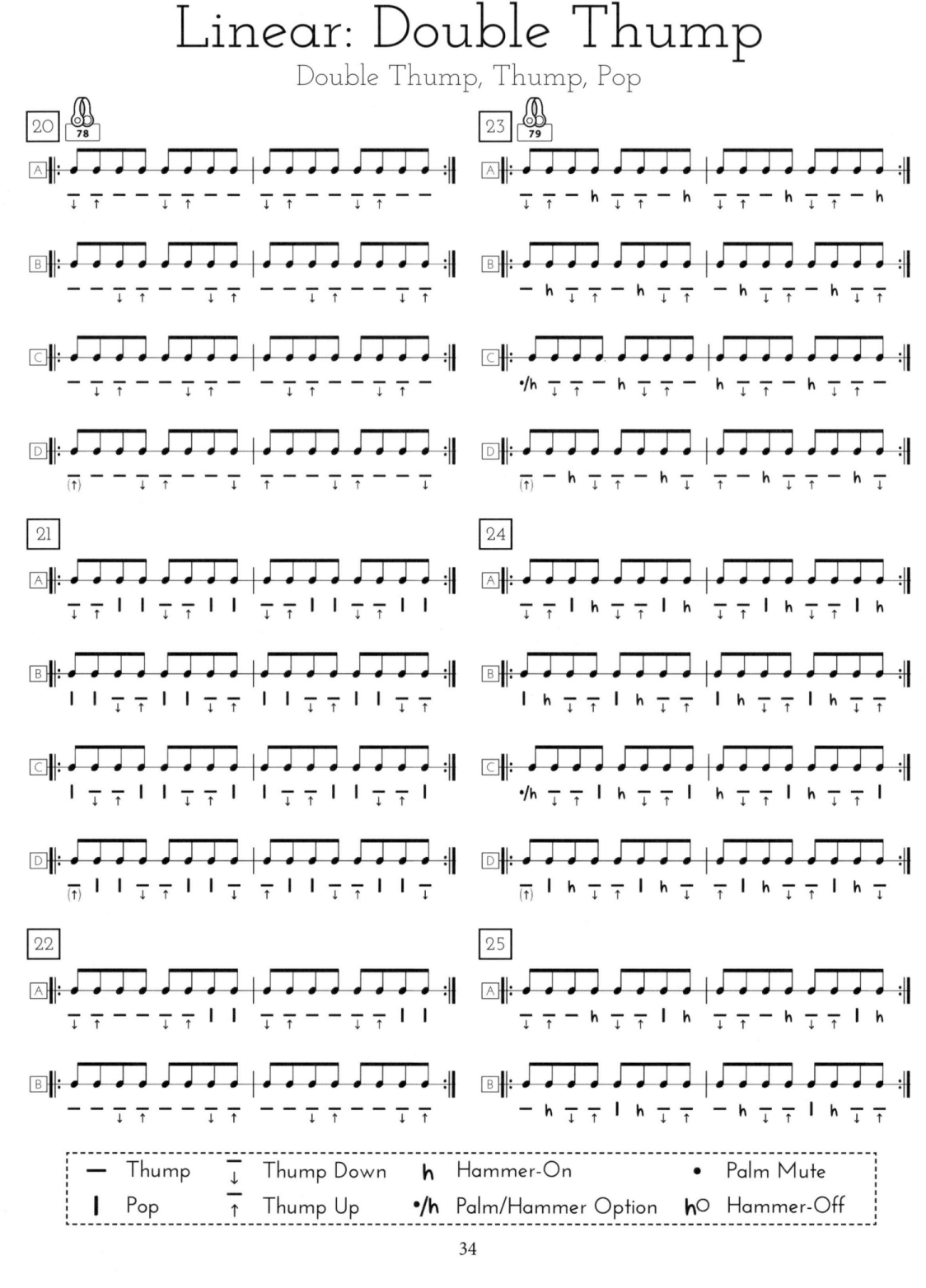

Linear: Double Thump

Double Thump, Thump, Pop

"If you believe in your art & you love what you do, that energy will go out & people will respond."
- *Ray Conniff*

"Play as much as you can as often as you can with as many people as you can. That's how you learn and grow."
- *Les Claypool*

"For a musician, it's important to follow your own heart and know what you want to do. Reading too many reviews or paying too much attention to what people say might get you confused or insecure."
- *Tobias Exxel*

"Guitar is for the head, drums are for the chest, but bass gets you in the groin."
- *Suzi Qatro*

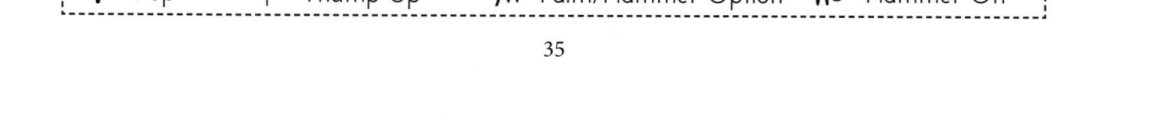

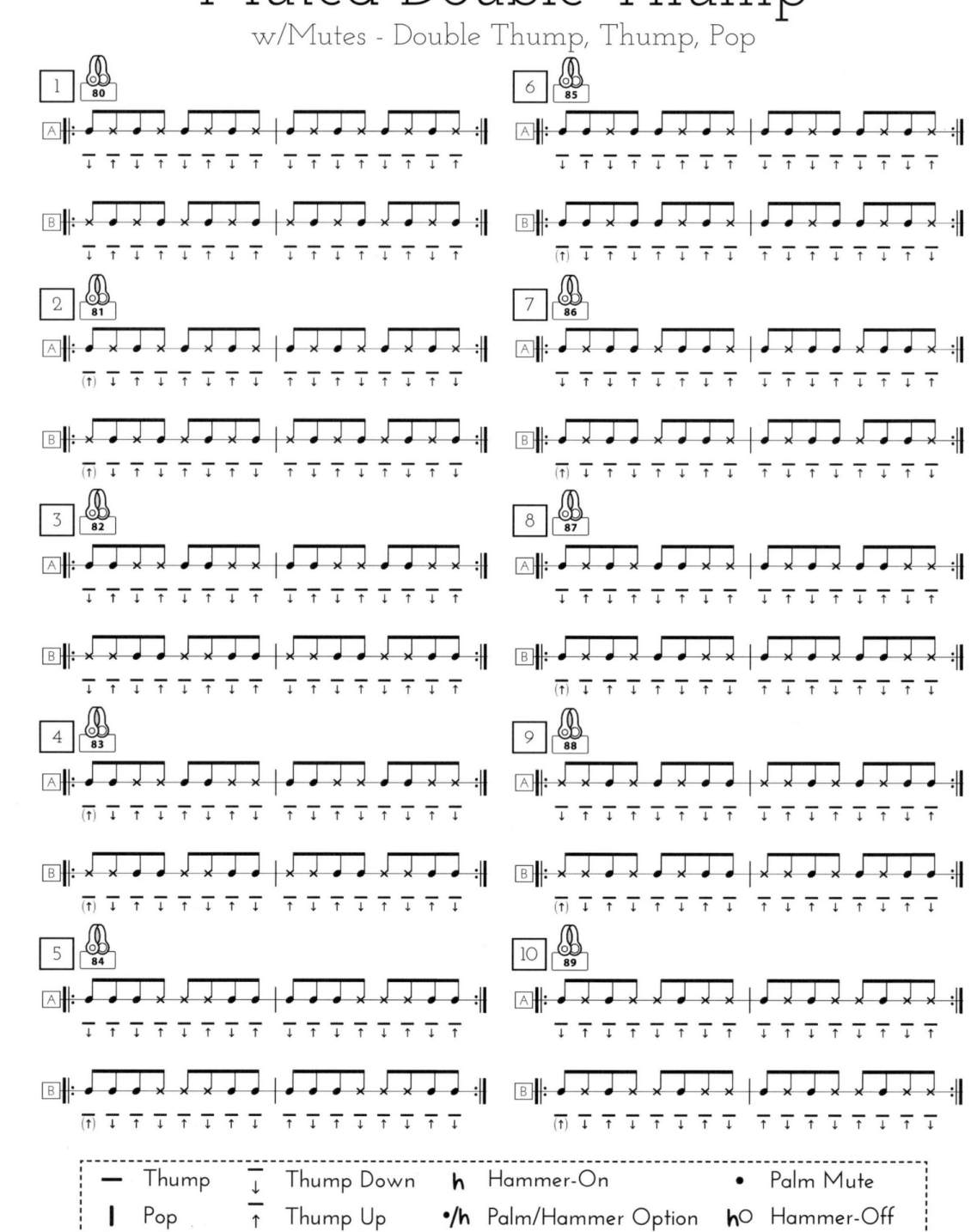

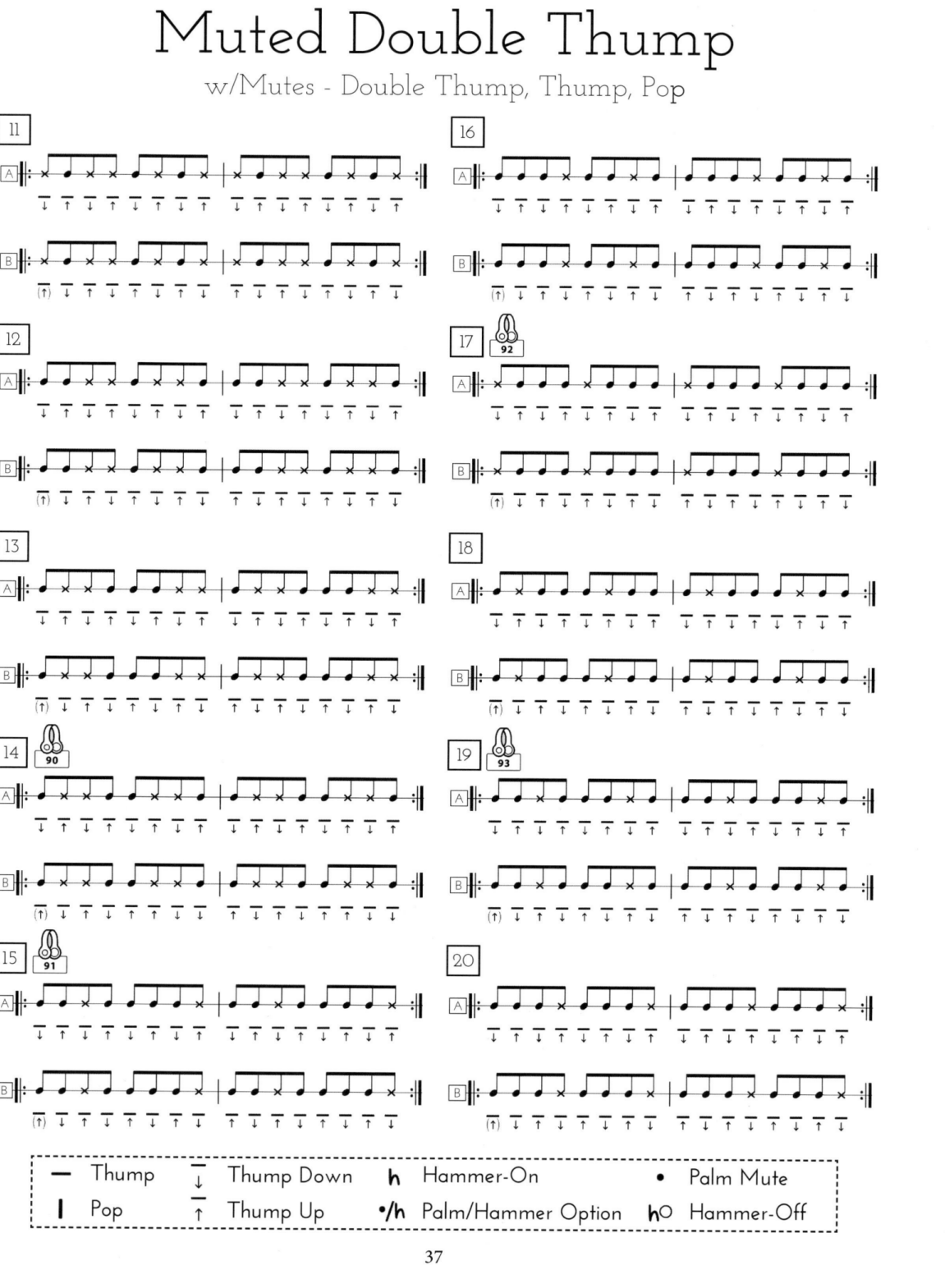

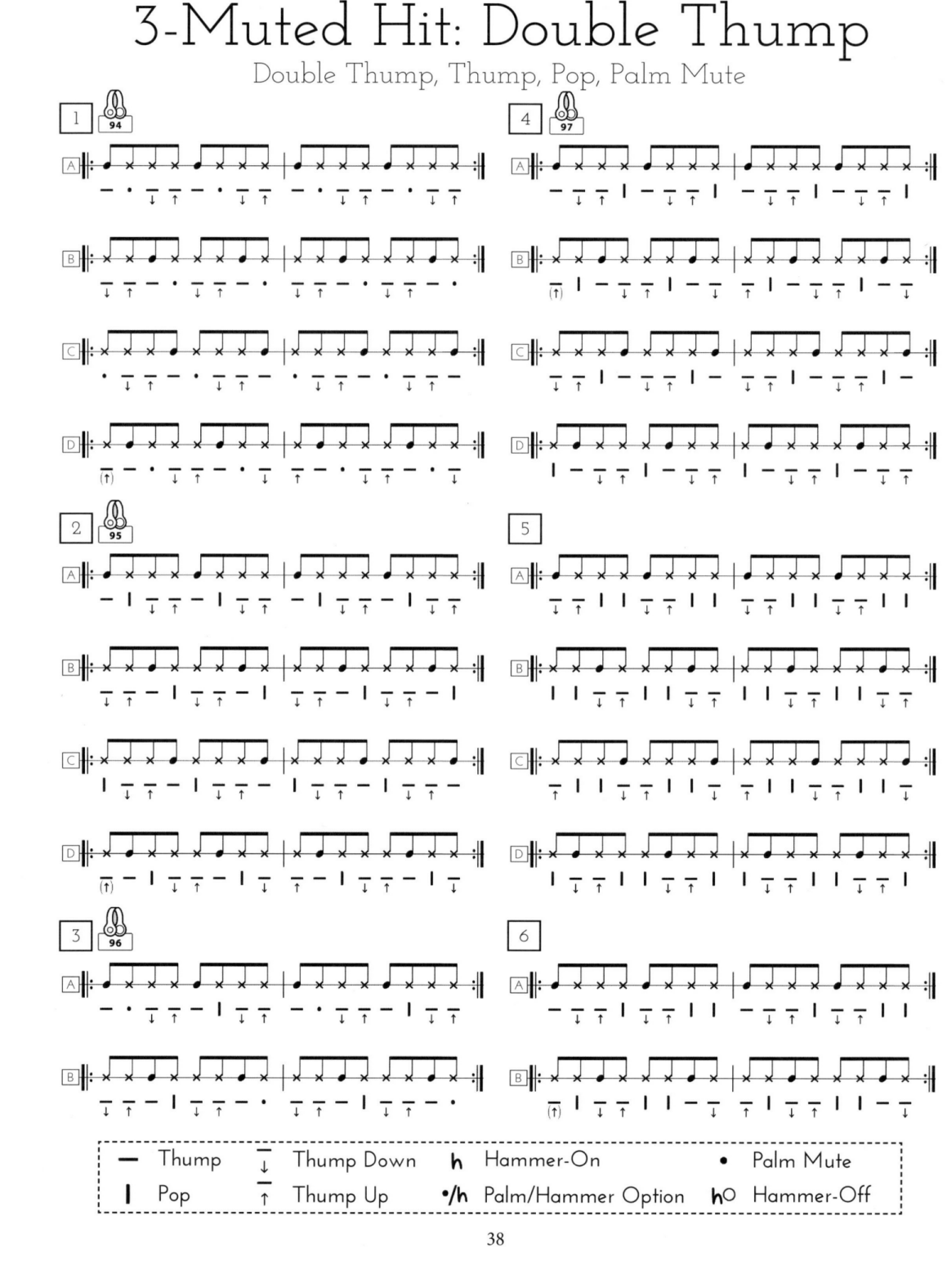

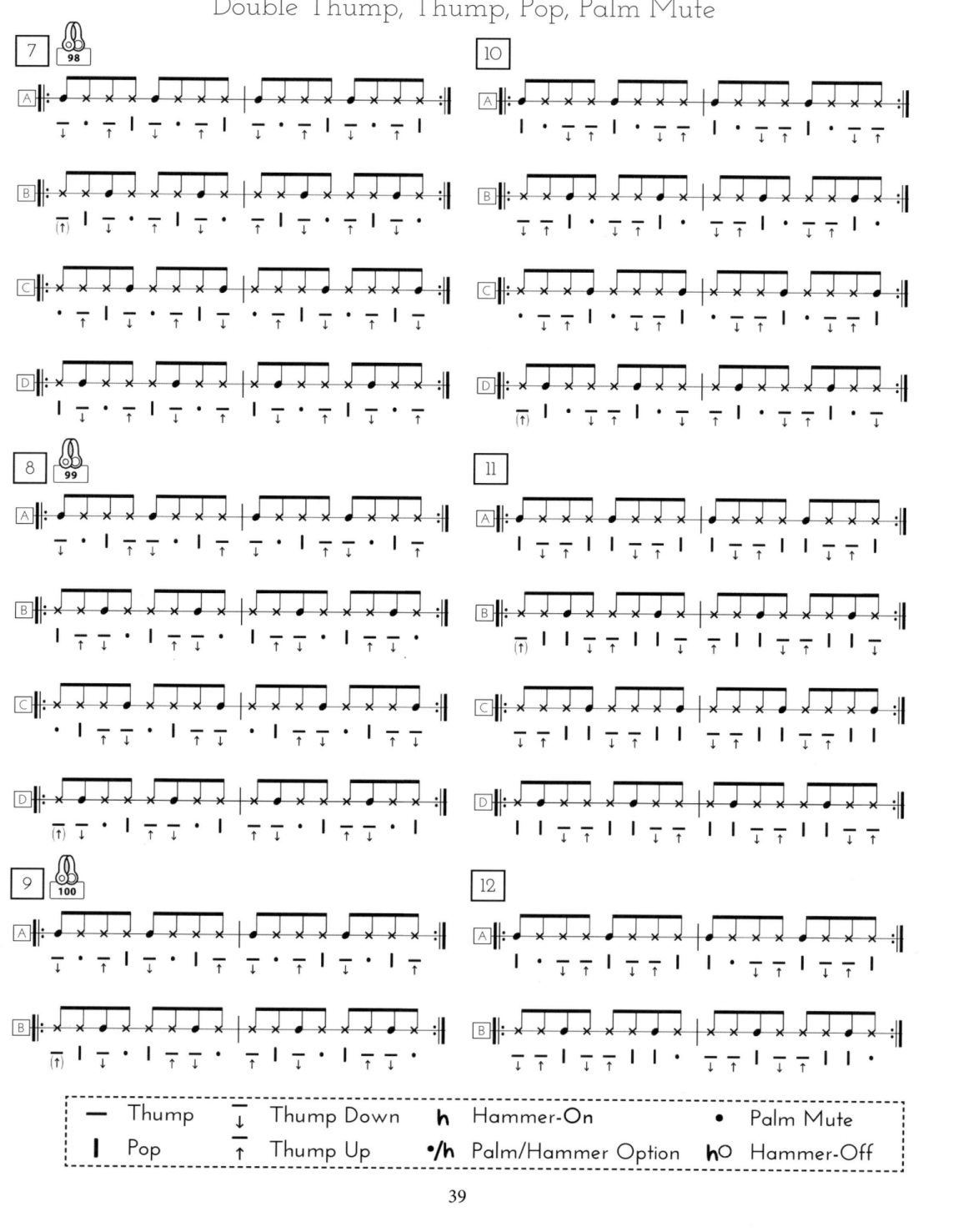

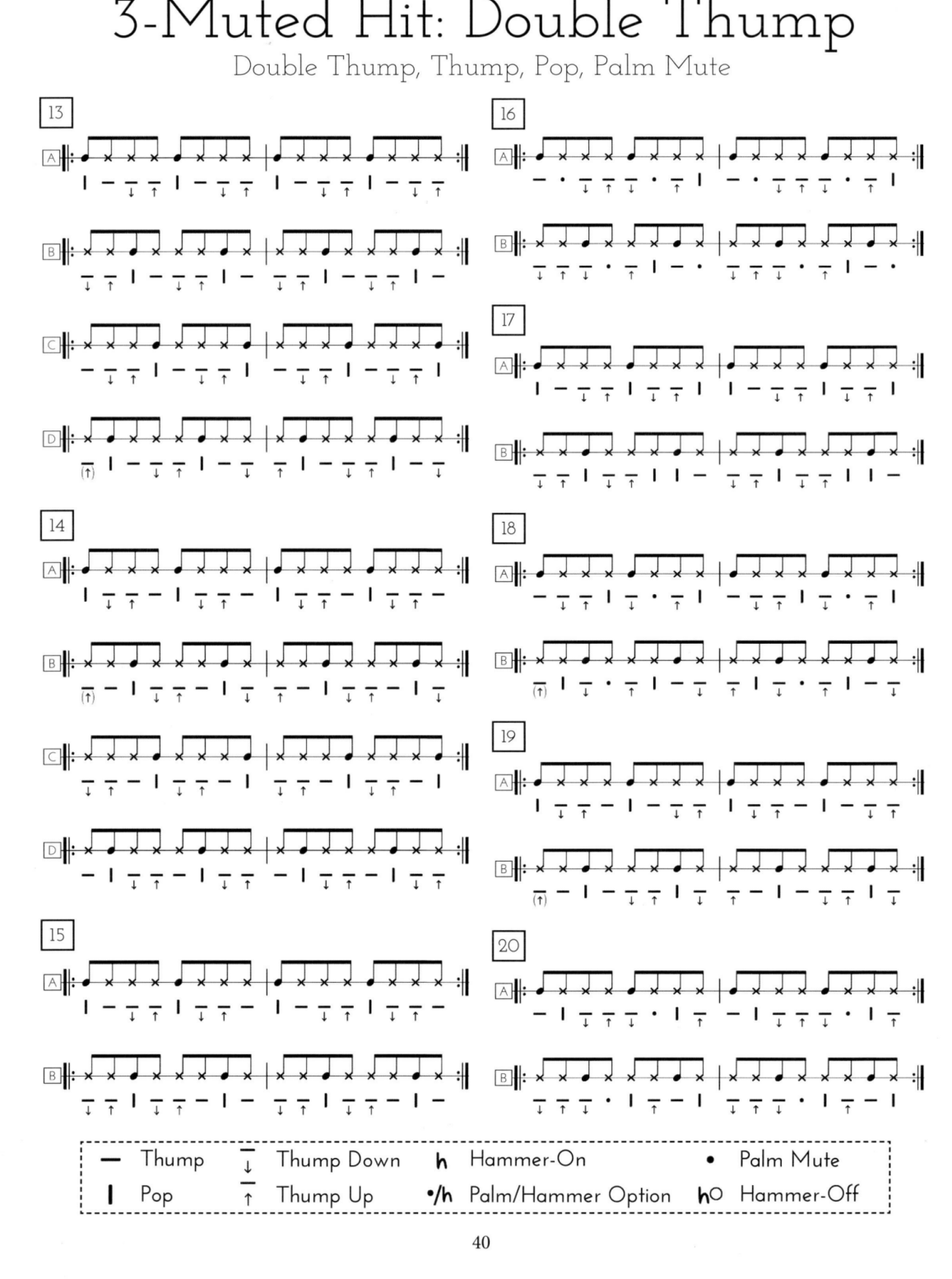

PARADIDDLES

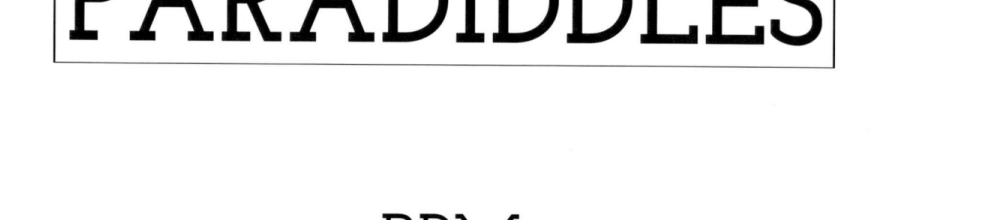

About This Section

These exercises are based on the "Paradiddle" snare rudiment (RRLR LLRL in snare notation) and contain thump, pop, double thump, and muted hits.

These rhythms are not just single paradiddles, however. In this section are single, double, and even triple paradiddles, as well as the inversions of each and some combinations of themselves.

Single Paradiddle: RLRR - LRLL

Double Paradiddle: RLRLRR - LRLRLL

Triple Paradiddle: RLRLRLRR - LRLRLRLL

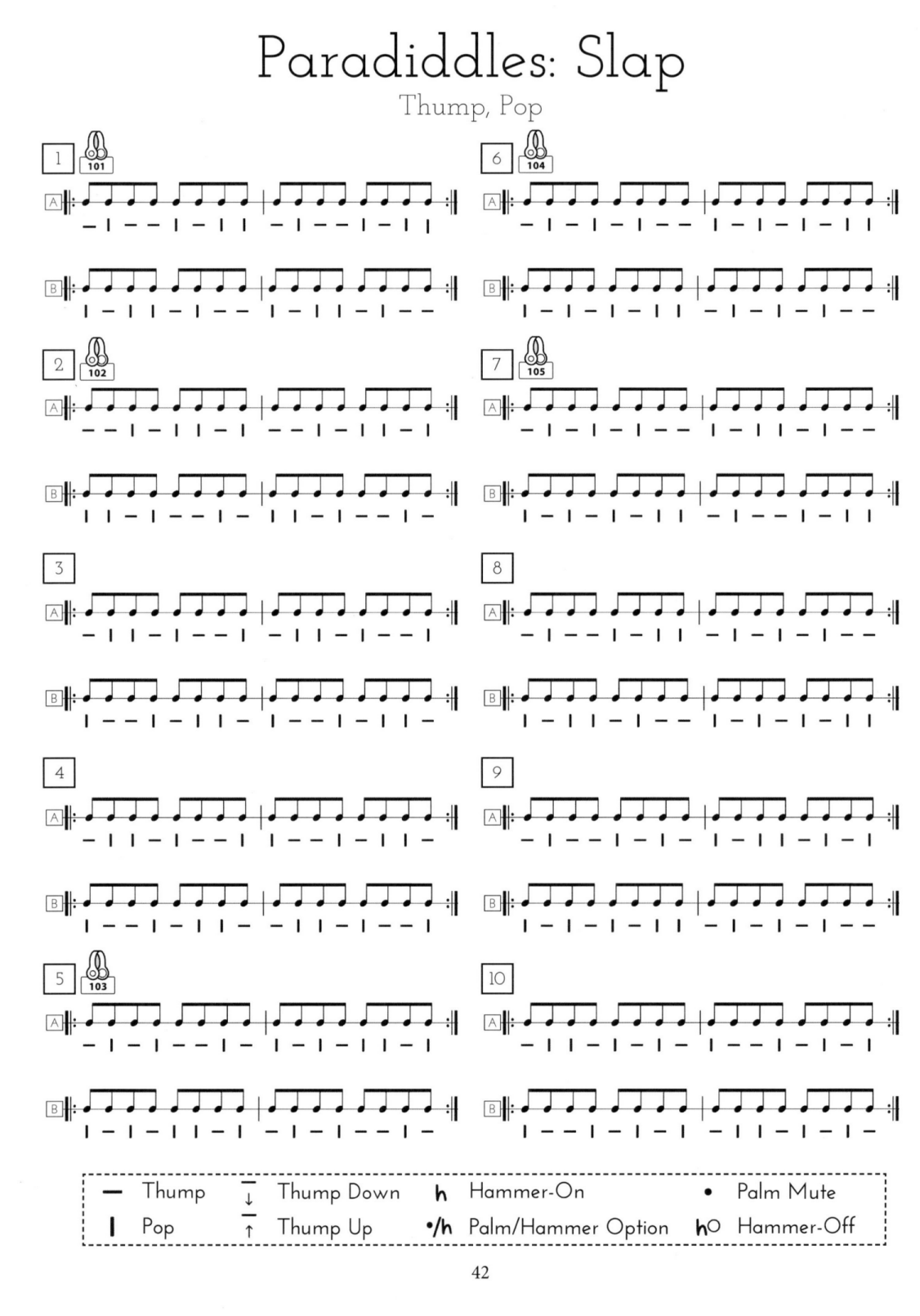

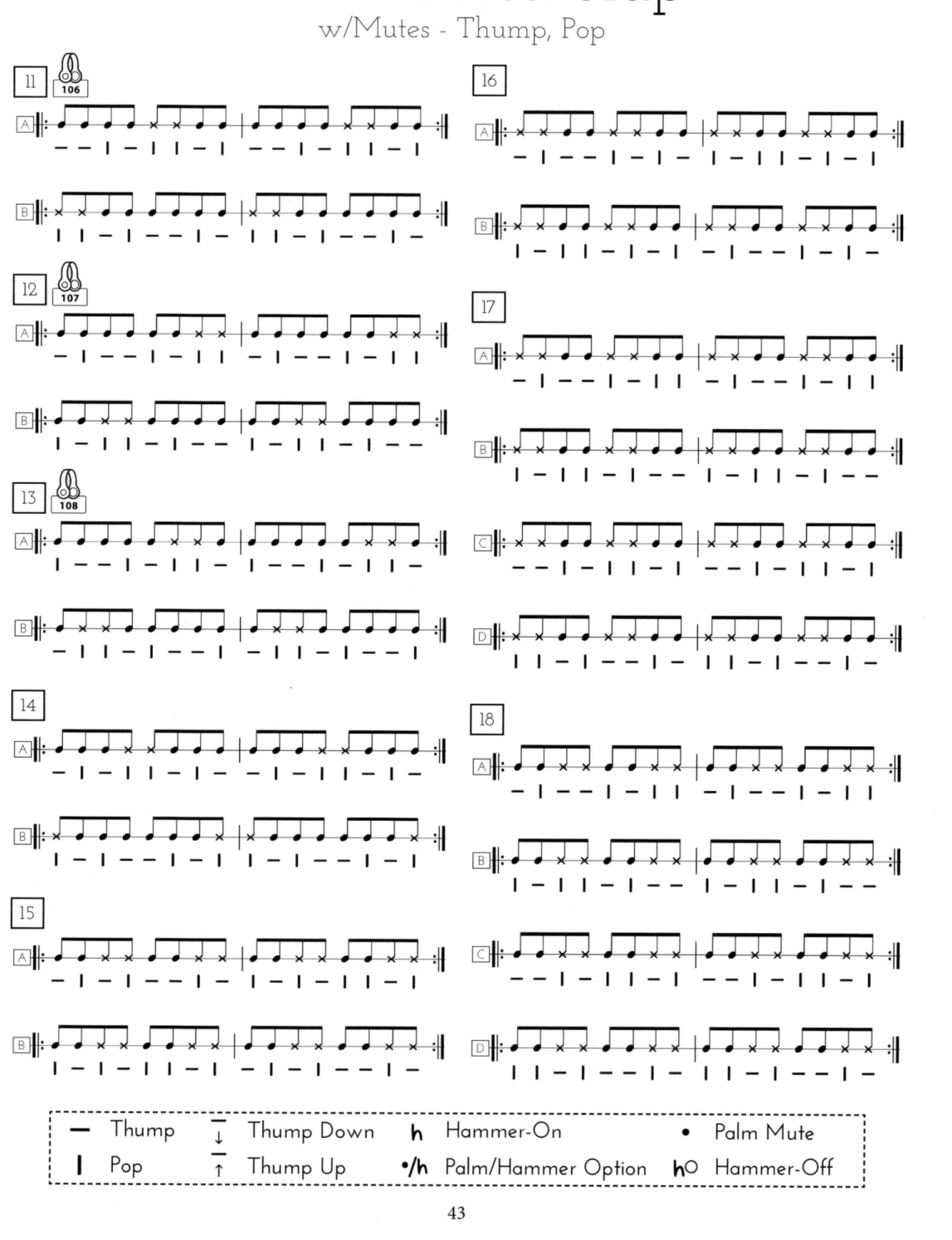

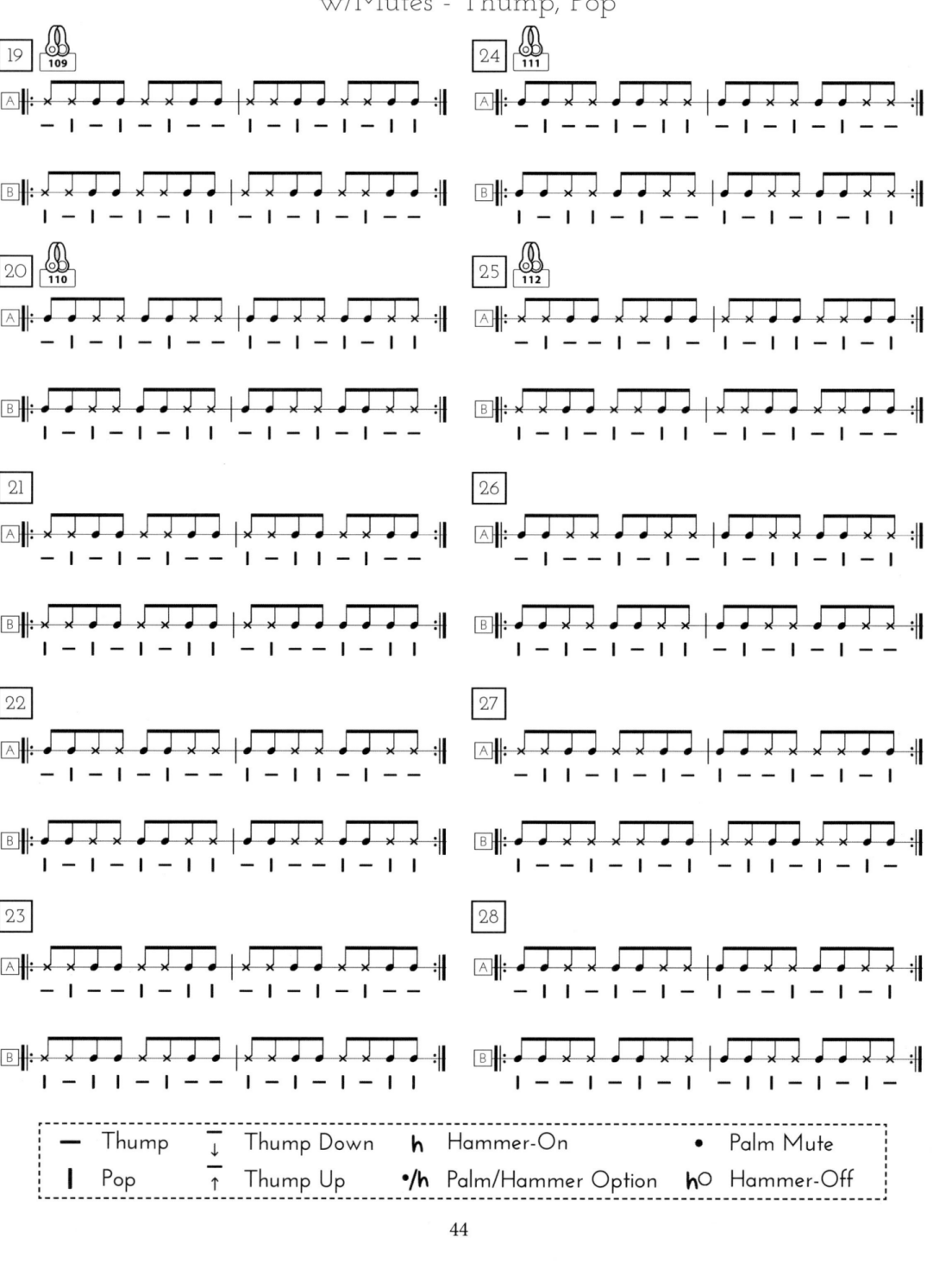

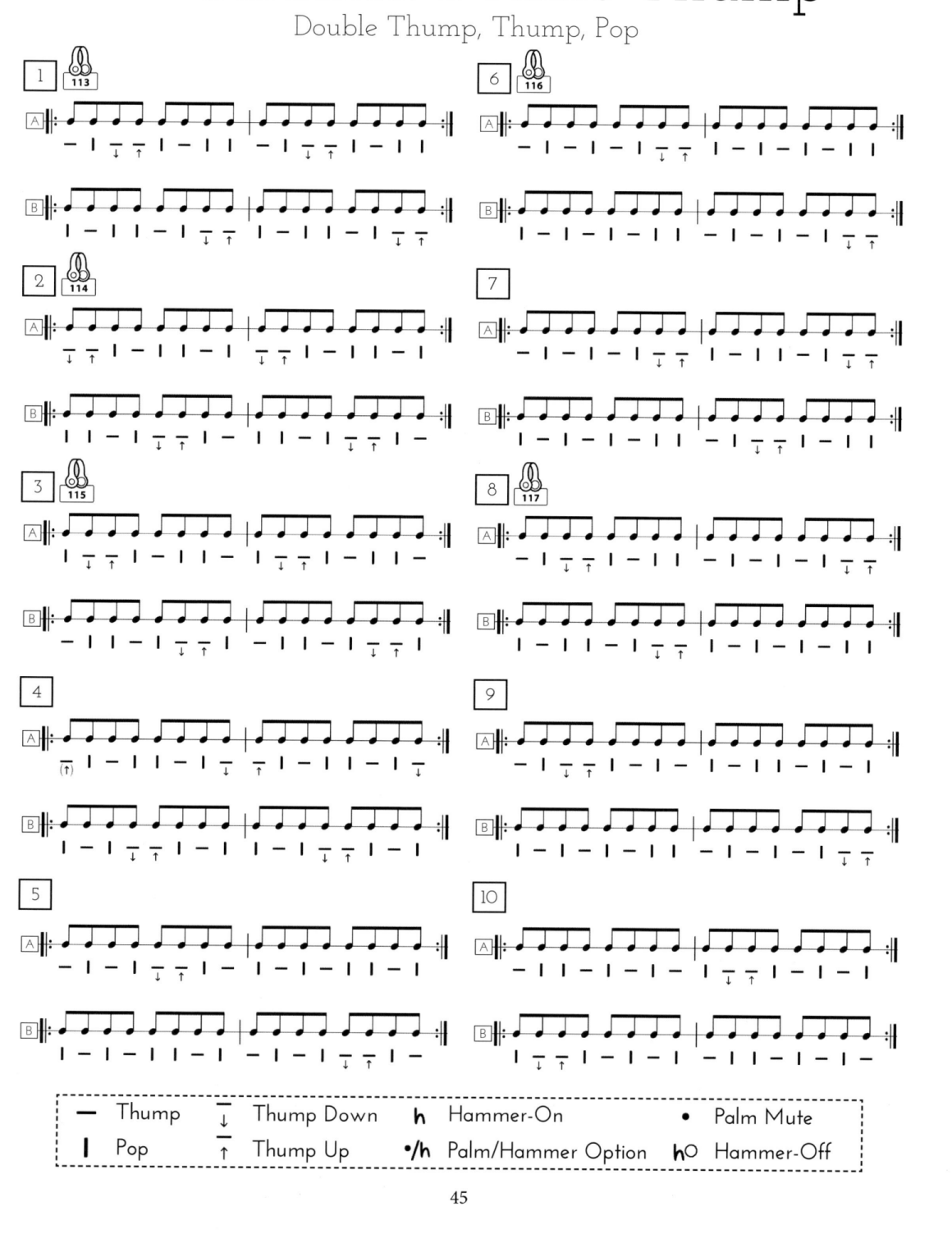

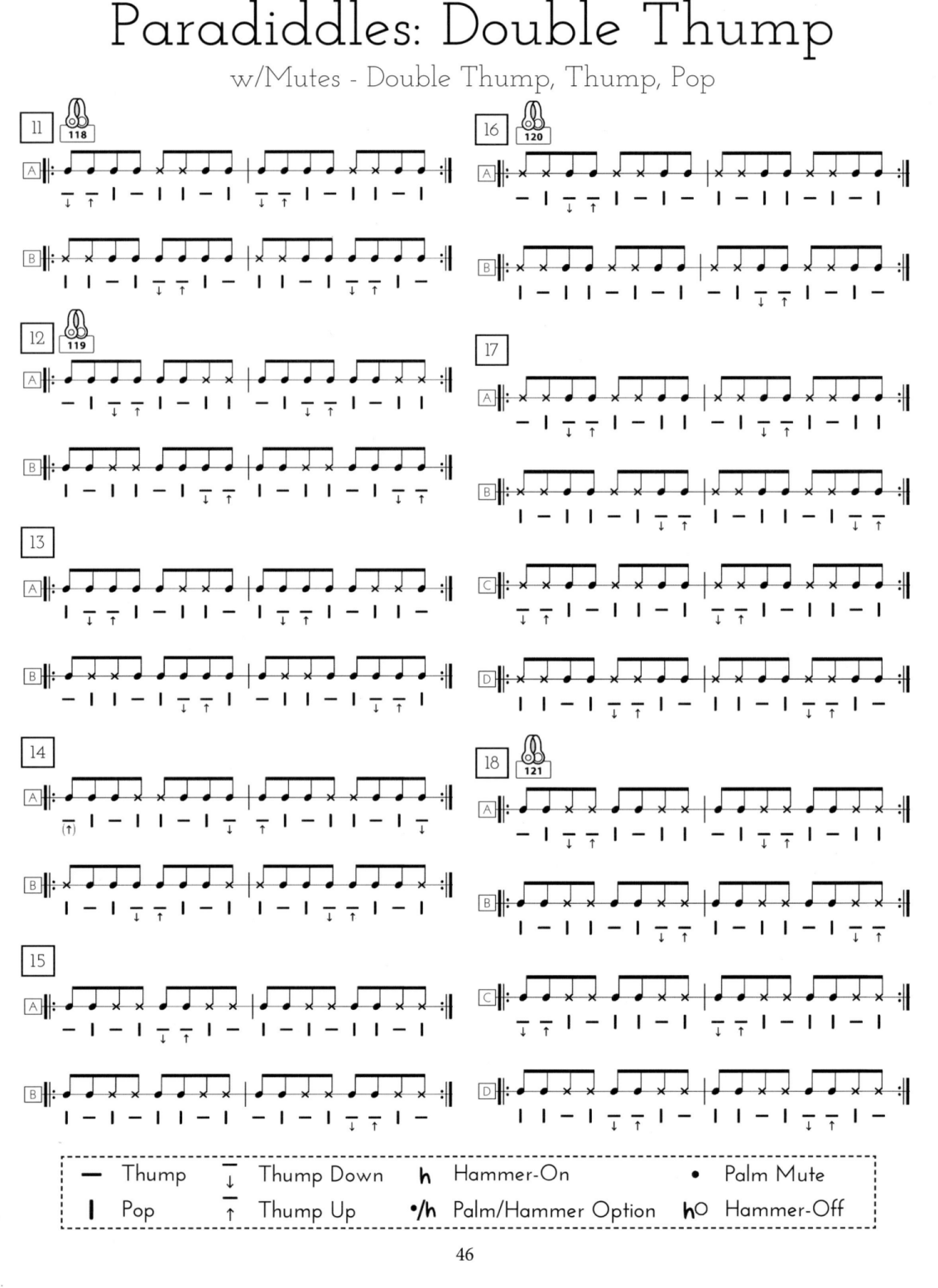

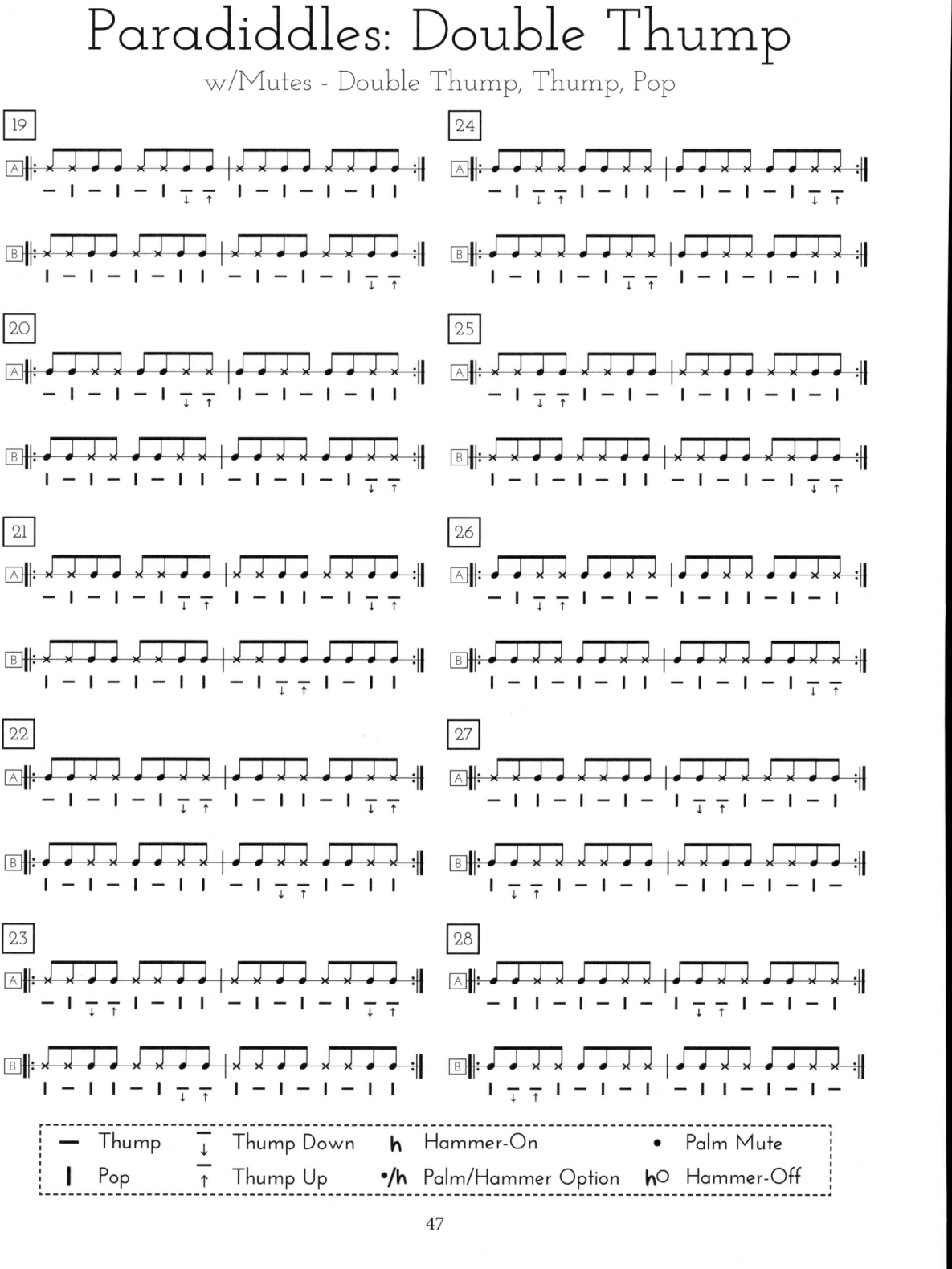

TRIPLETS

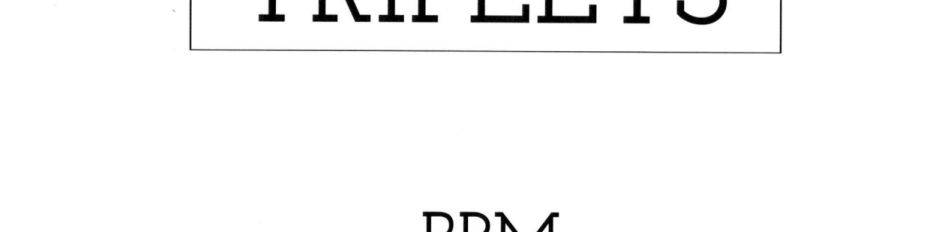

About This Section

The exercises in this section are all Triplets, or groups of hits subdivided into 3 instead of 2 (known as a duplet). This section features every type of hit: Thump, Pop, Double Thump, Hammer-On/Off, Palm Mutes, and Muted hits.

Triplet rhythms in this section are assigned a 2/4 time signature and feature 6 (triplet) eighth notes every measure.

Also contained in this section are "Triplet-Ta's": patterns of 4 notes that contain a triplet followed or preceded by a quarter note.

1st Variation Triplet-Ta: Triplet - 1/4 note

2nd Variation Triplet-Ta: 1/4 note - Triplet

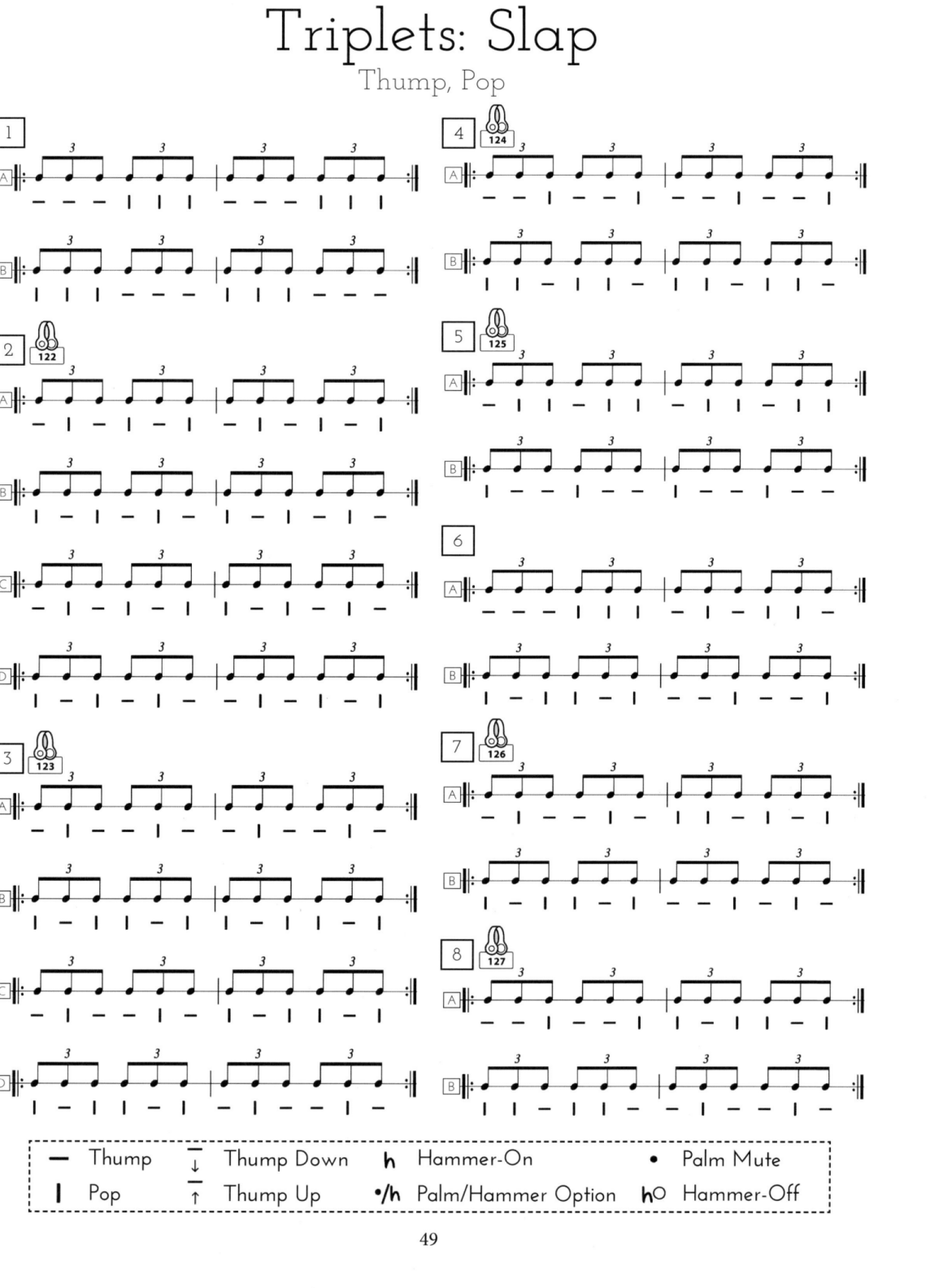

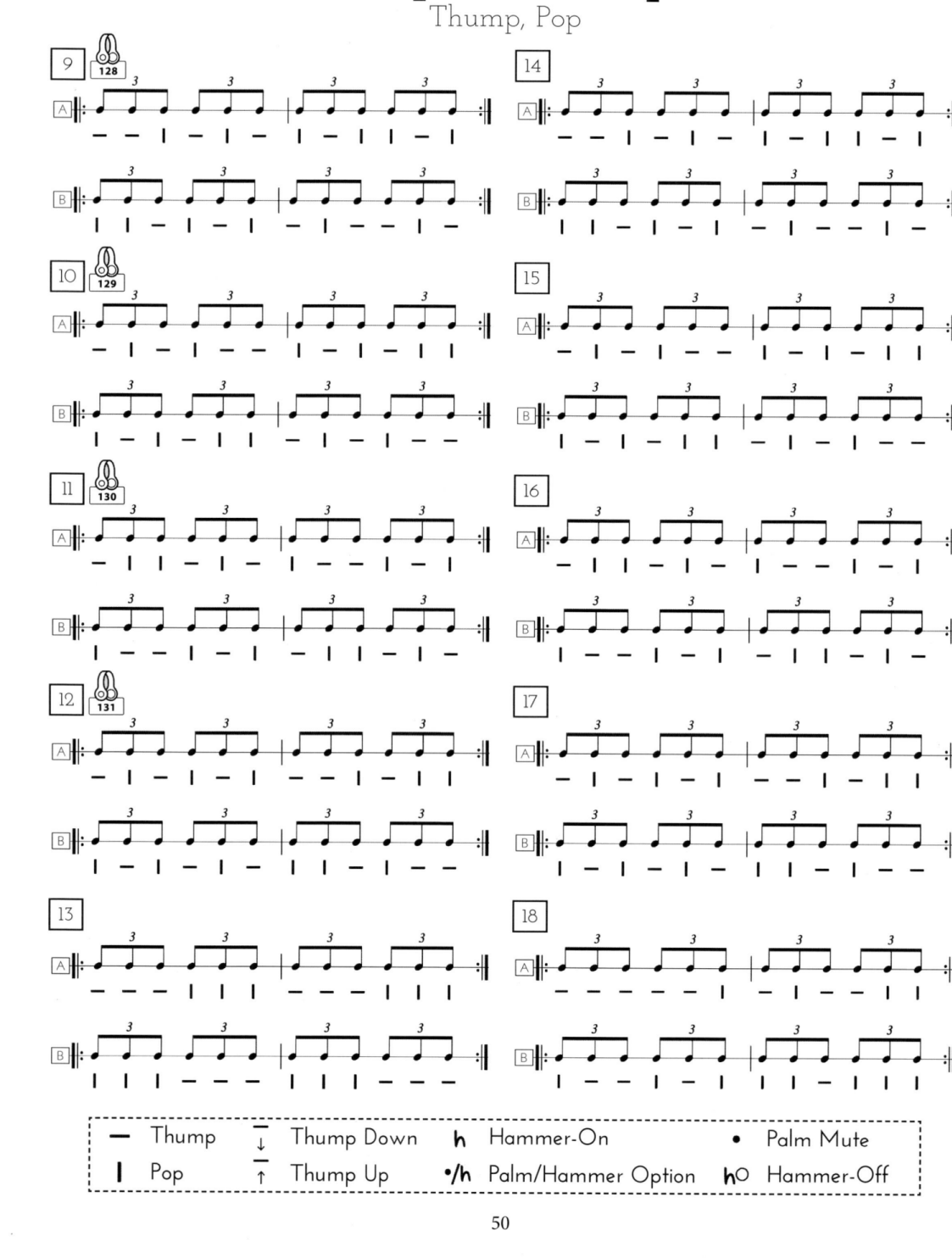

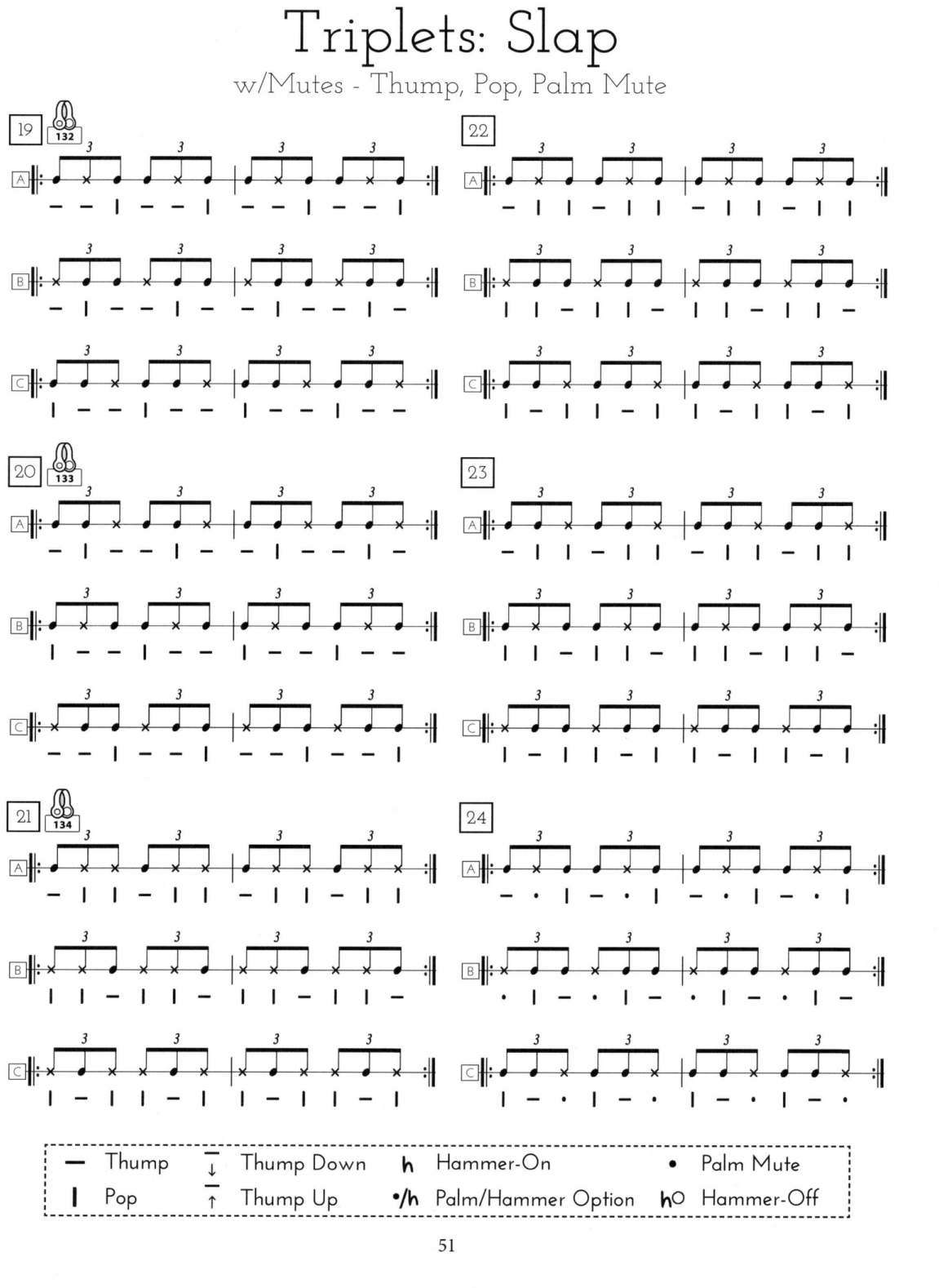

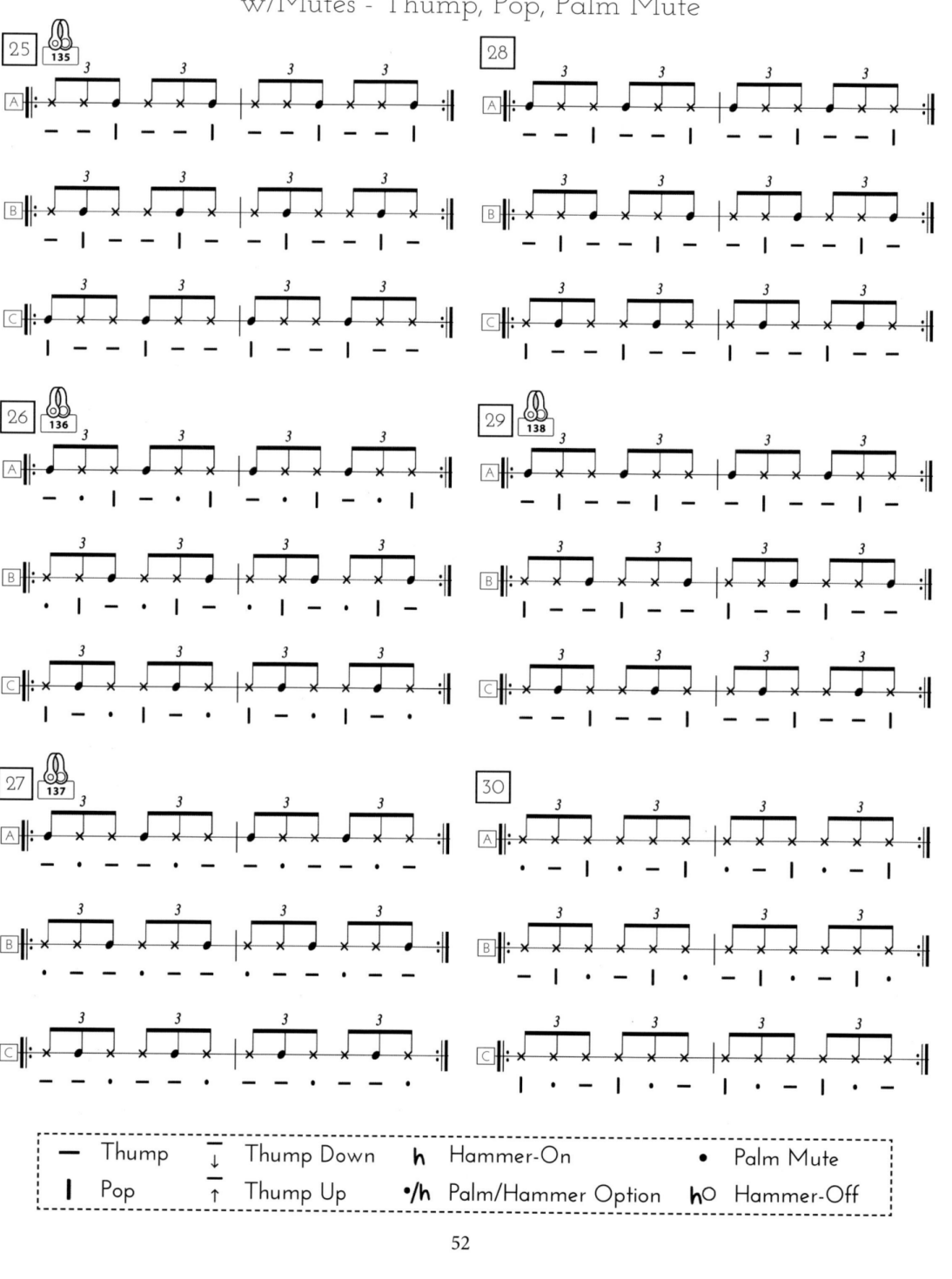

Triplets: Slap

Thump, Pop, Hammer-On/Off

"It's really easy to play harmonics, anyone can do it. It's another thing to be able to swing, to make to make a band swing, to create a groove. Cleverness is no substitute for true awareness."

- *Jaco Pastorius*

"...The checks and balances are the same: The drums are the executive branch. The jazz orchestra is the legislative branch. Logic and reason are like jazz solos... The bass player is the judicial branch."

- *Wynton Marsalis*

"None of us wanted to be the bass player. In our minds he was the fat guy who always played at the back"

- *Paul McCartney*

"Invest yourself in everything you do. There's fun in being serious."

- *John Coltrane*

"Imagine if you were a drummer, and you accidentally picked up two magic wands instead of sticks. There you are, keeping the beat, the next thing you know, your bass player turns into a can of soup."

- *Mitch Hedberg*

"Success isn't always about greatness. It's about consistency. Consistent hard work leads to success. Greatness will come."

- *Dwayne Johnson*

"Have no fear of perfection. You'll never reach it."

- *Salvador Dali*

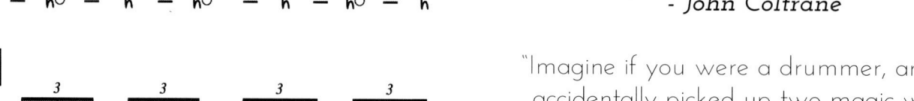

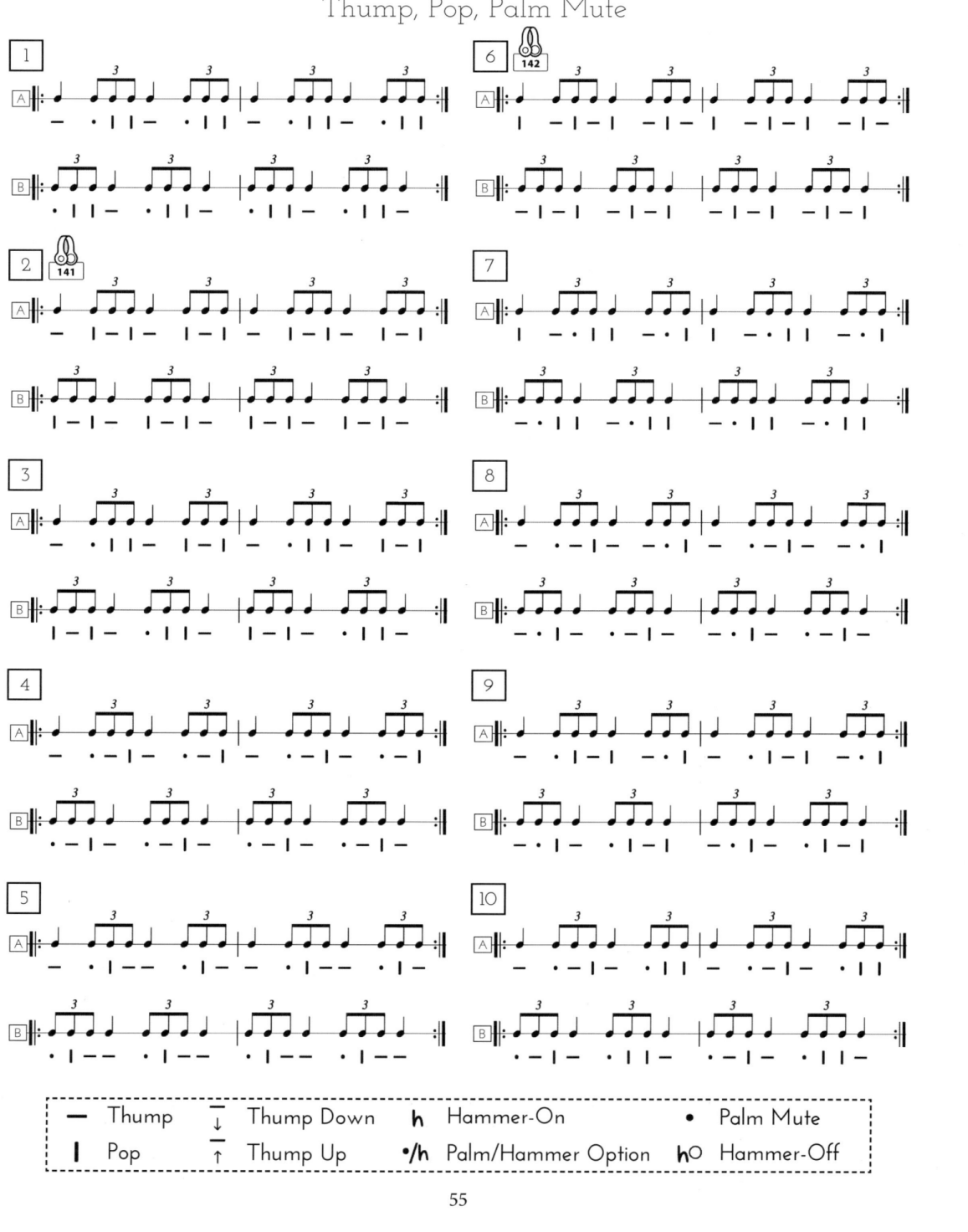

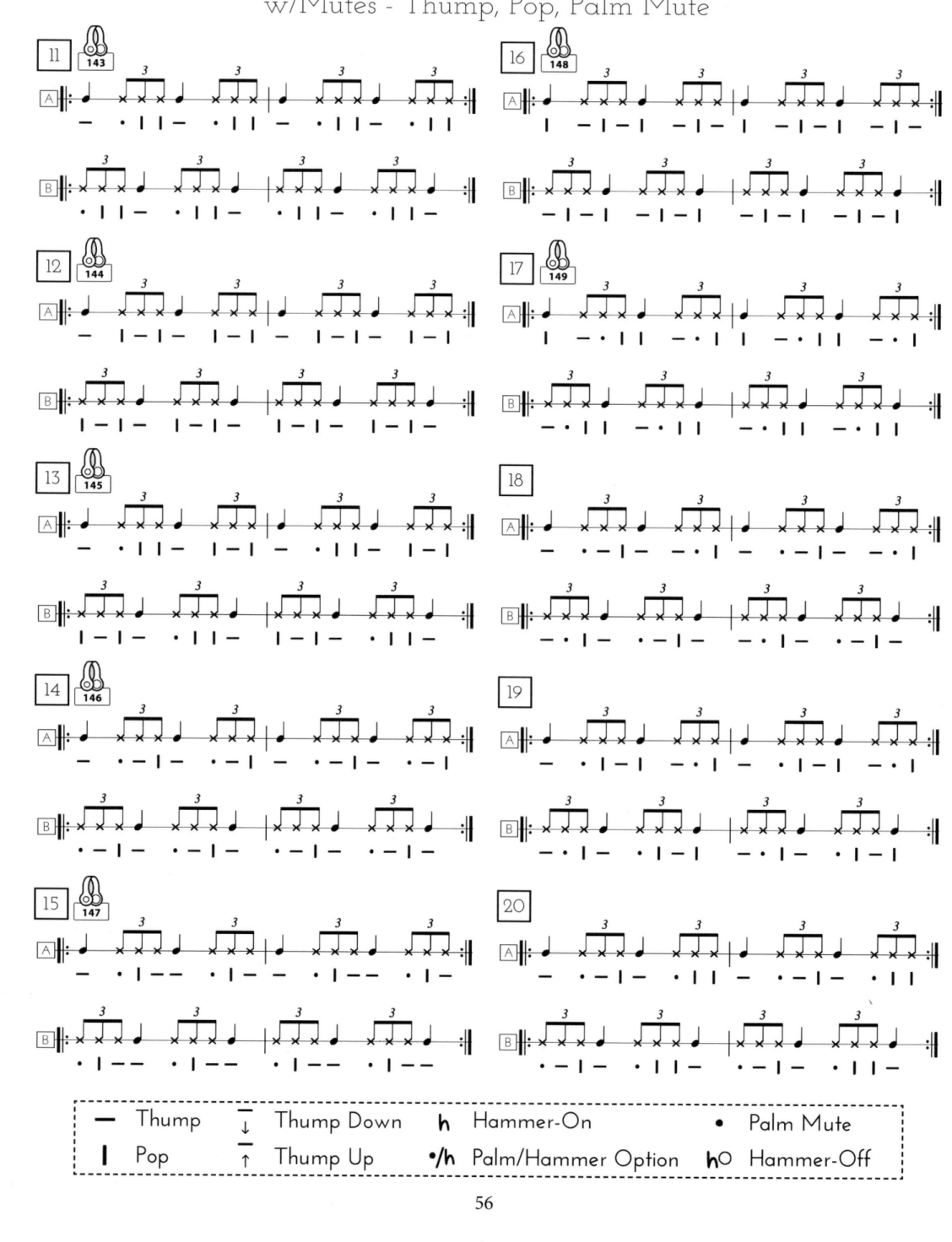

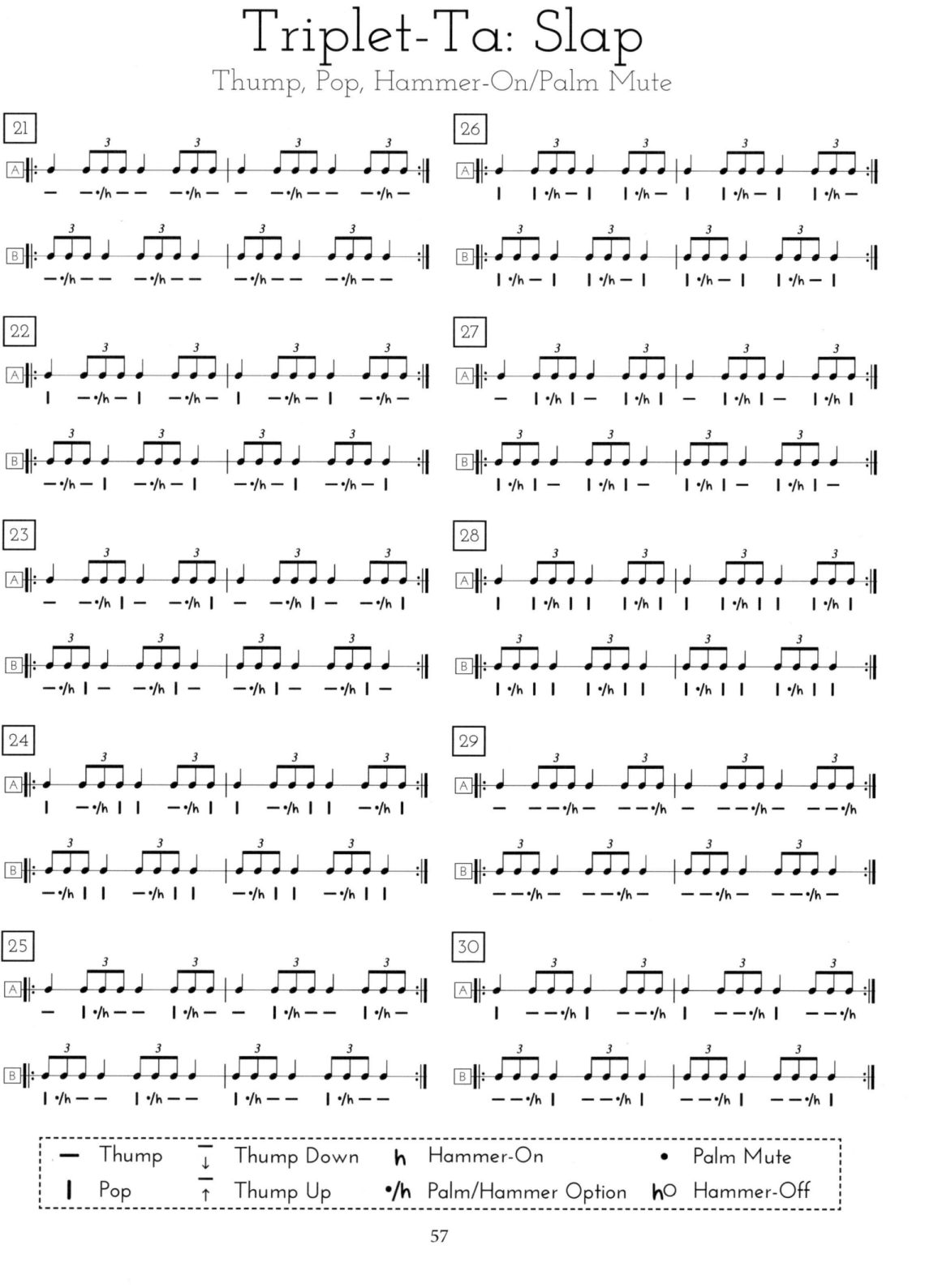

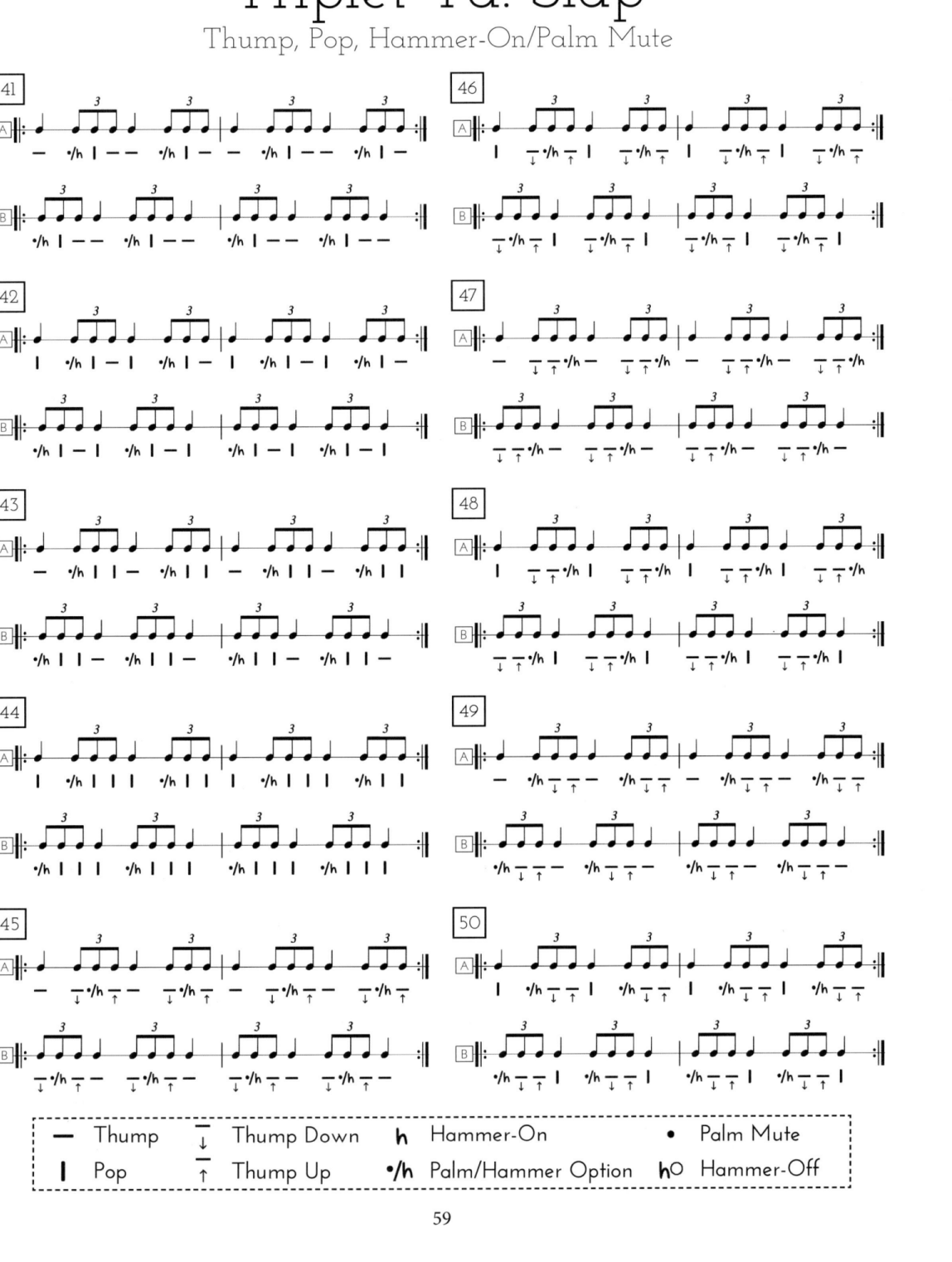

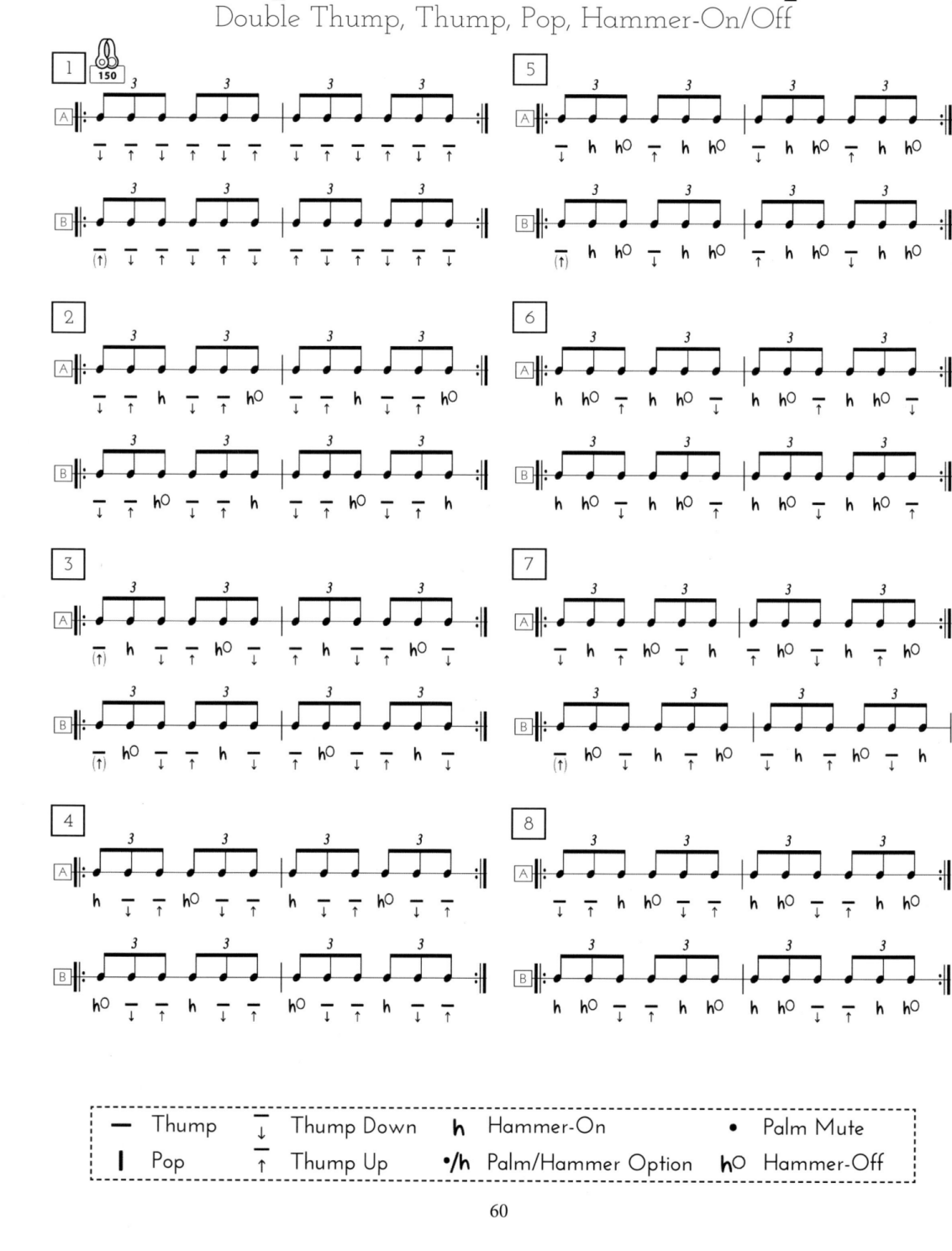

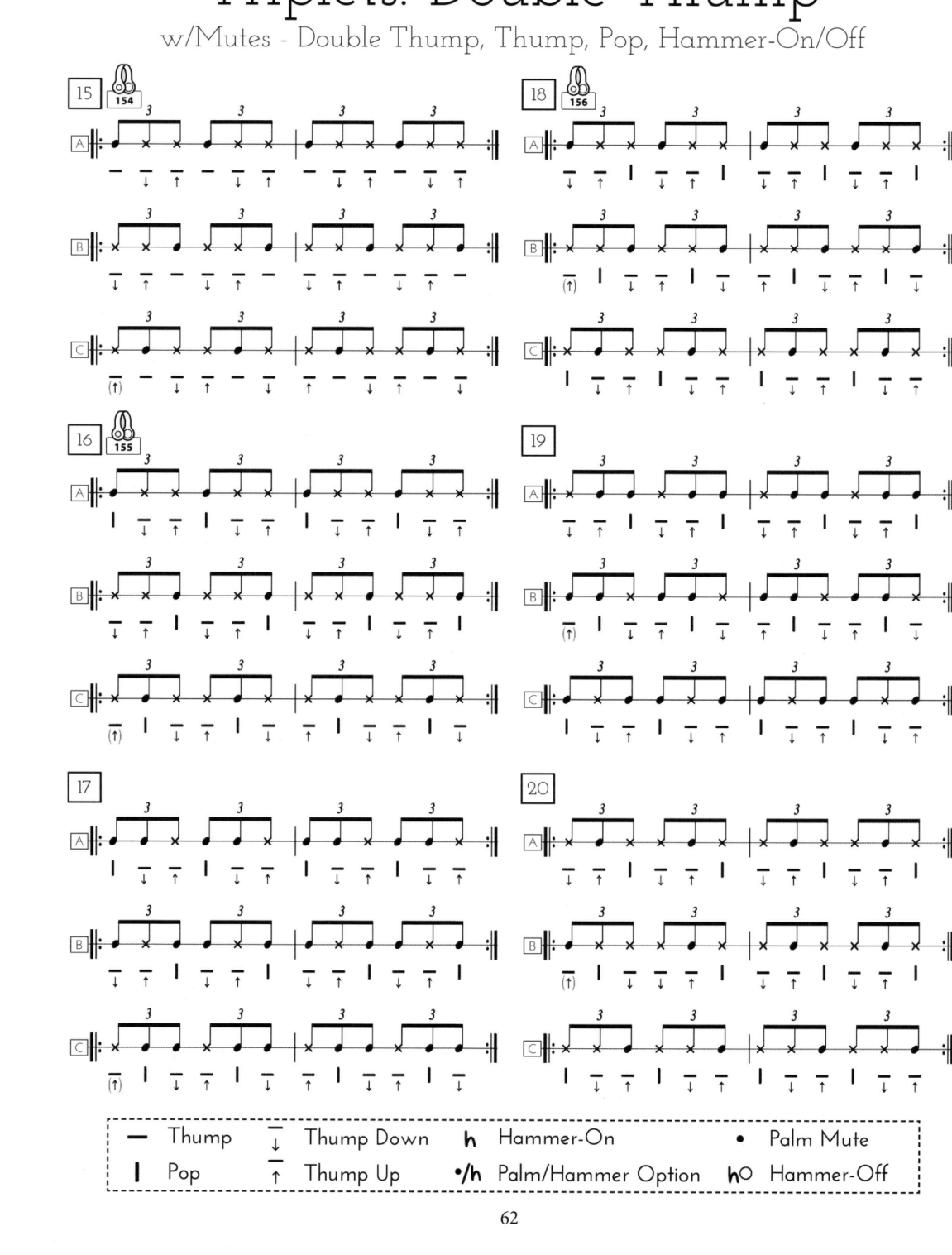

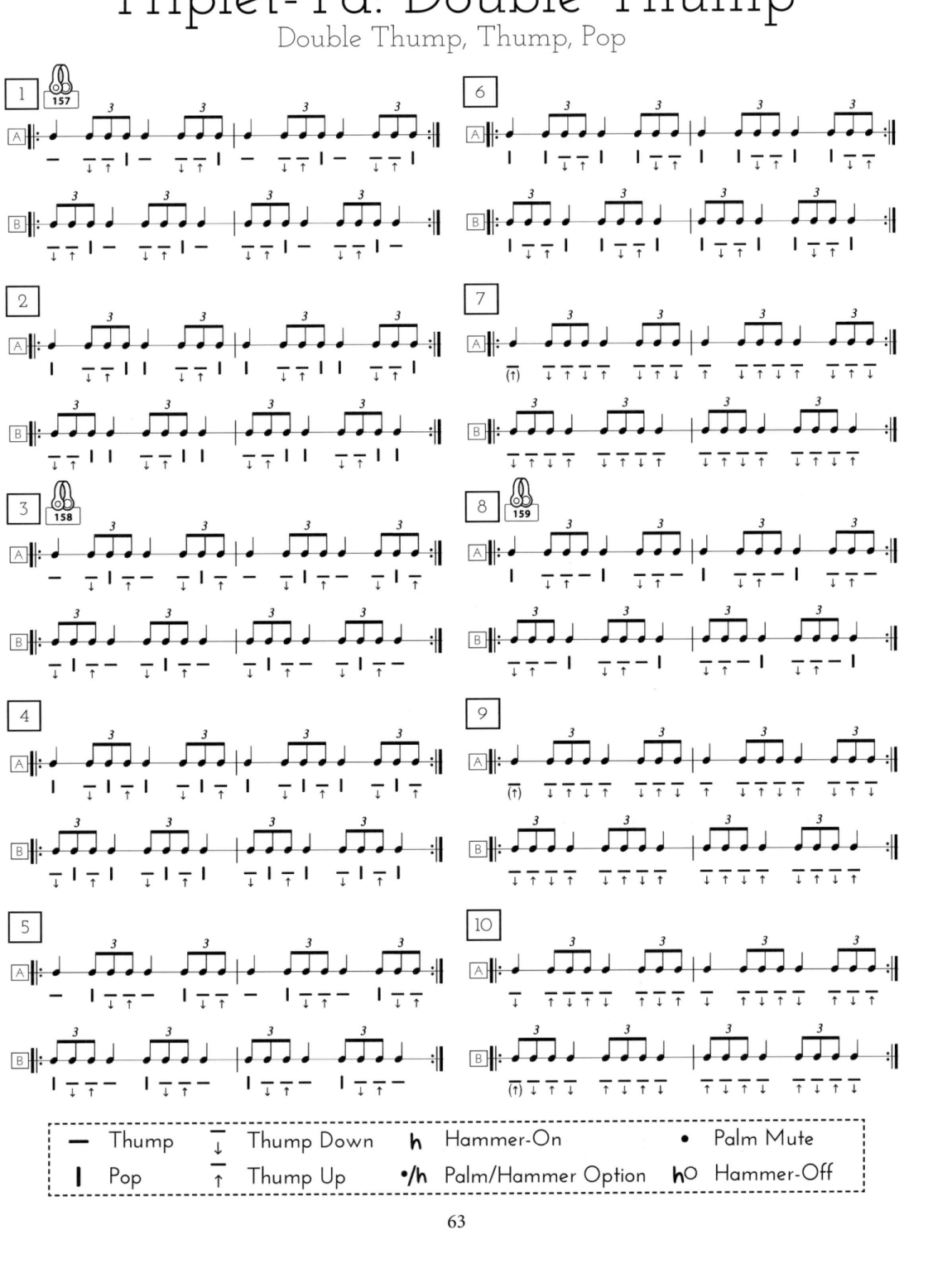

KHALIGI

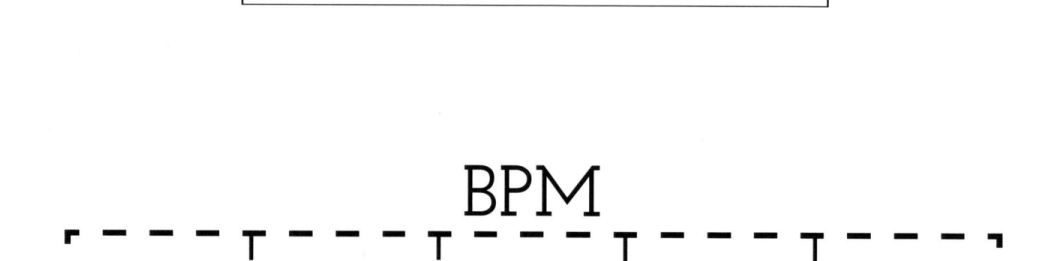

About This Section

The exercises in this section are called Khaligis, an Eastern rhythm that features a measure of 8 eight notes subdivided into 3 groups of 3, 3, and 2. This section contains every type of hit: Thump, Pop, Double Thump, Hammer-On/Off, Palm Mutes, and Muted hits.

Khaligis are found in 3 different combinations and every exercises in this section will reflect as such:

1st Variation: 3 - 3 - 2

2nd Variation: 3 - 2 - 3

3rd Variation: 2 - 3 - 3

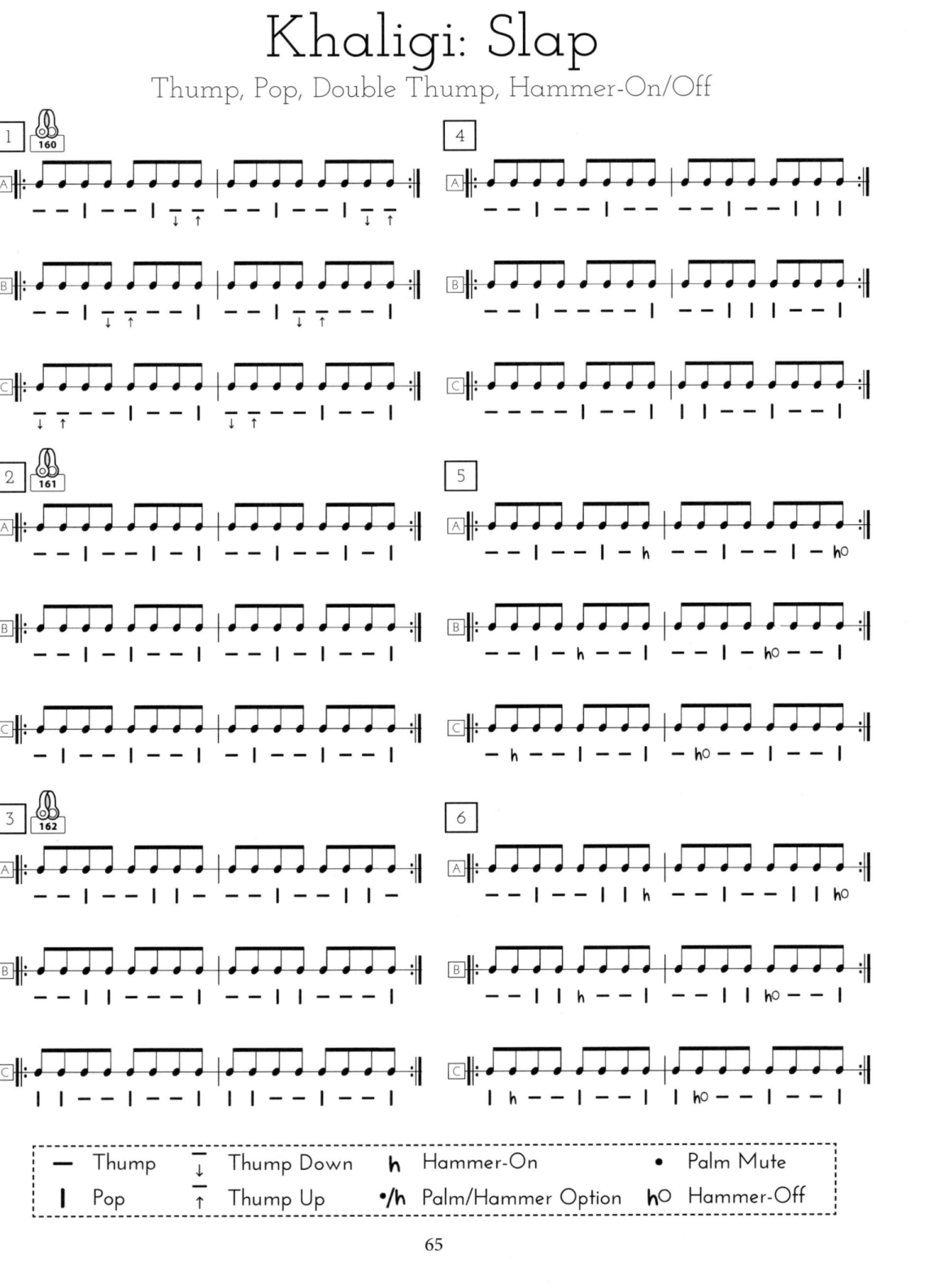

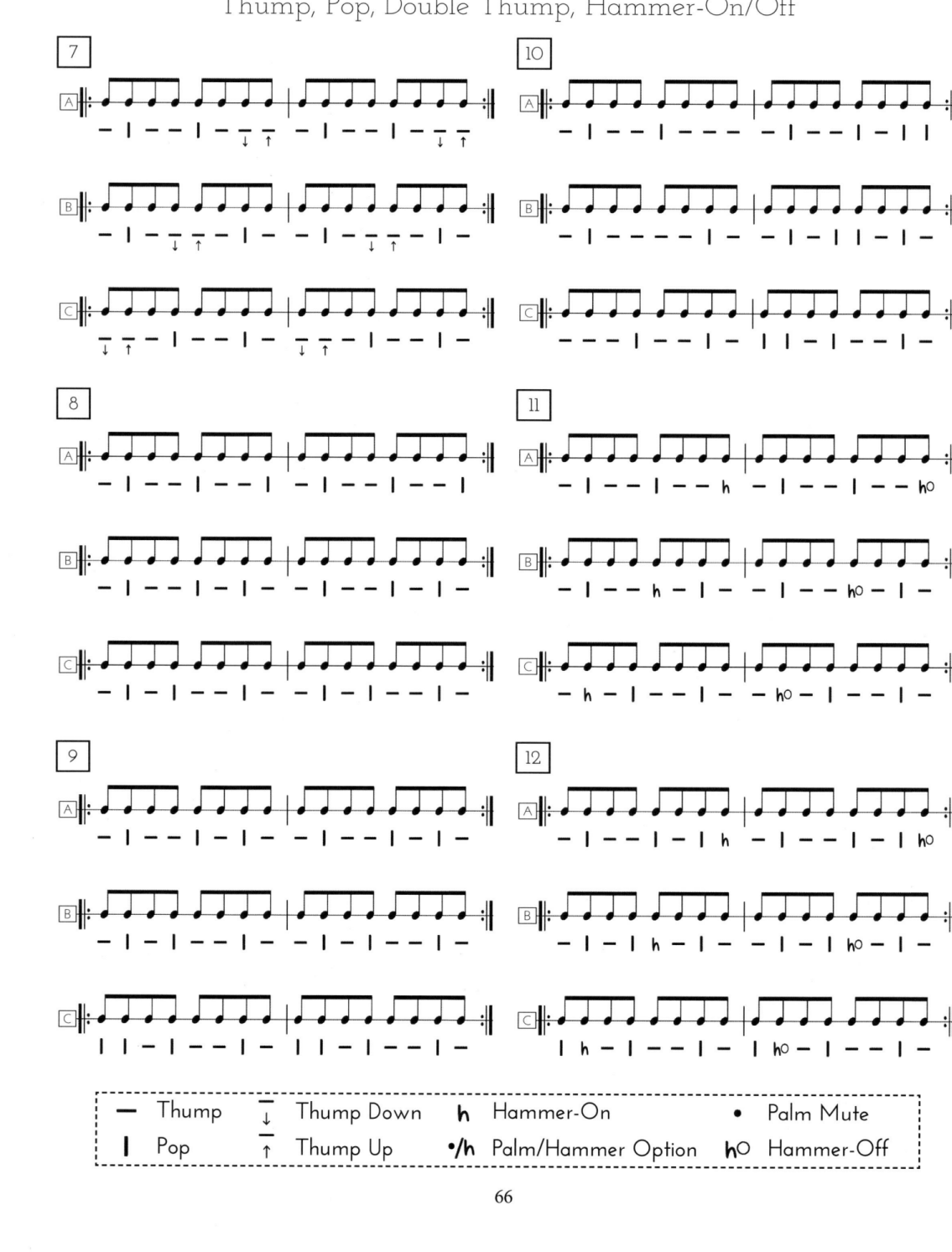

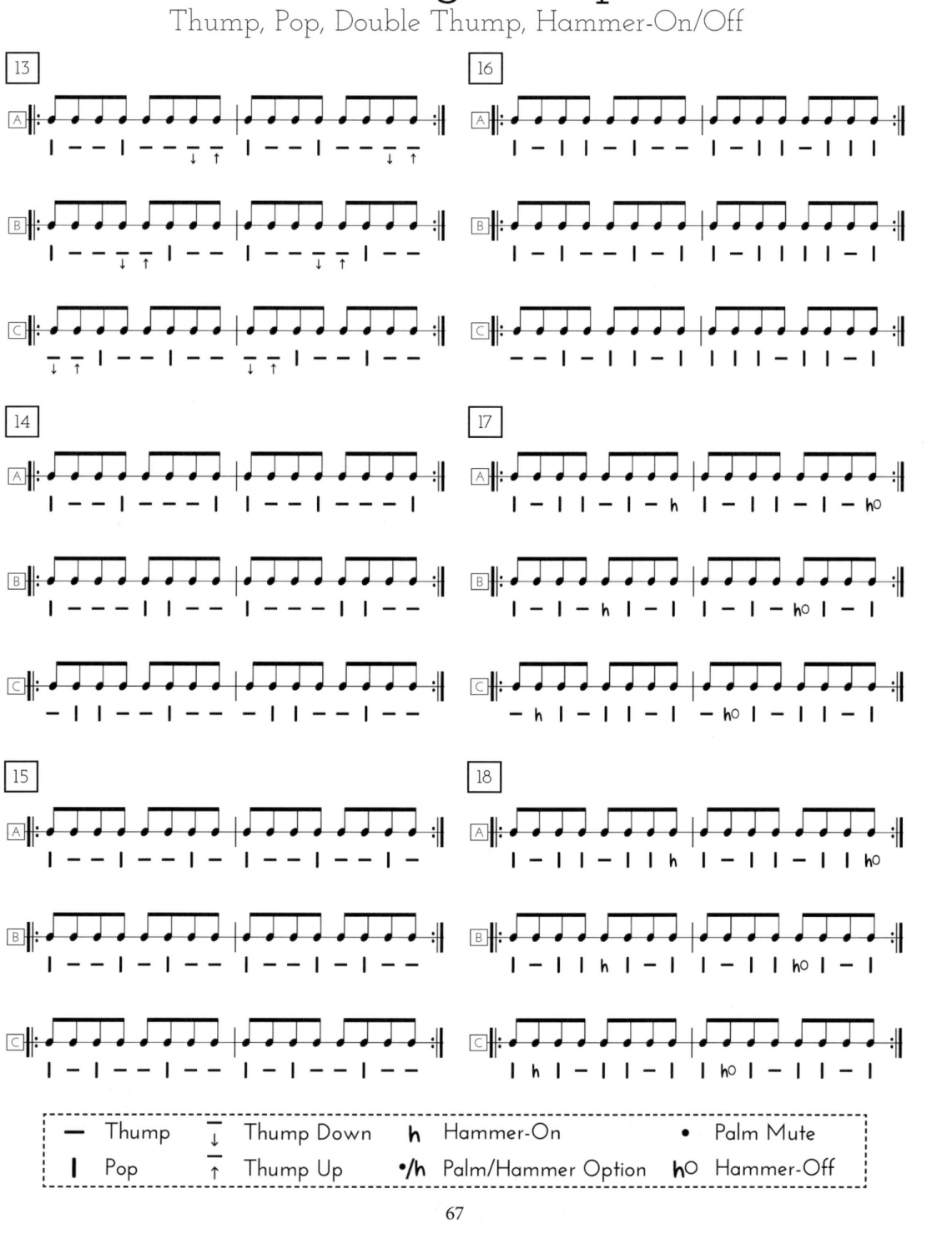

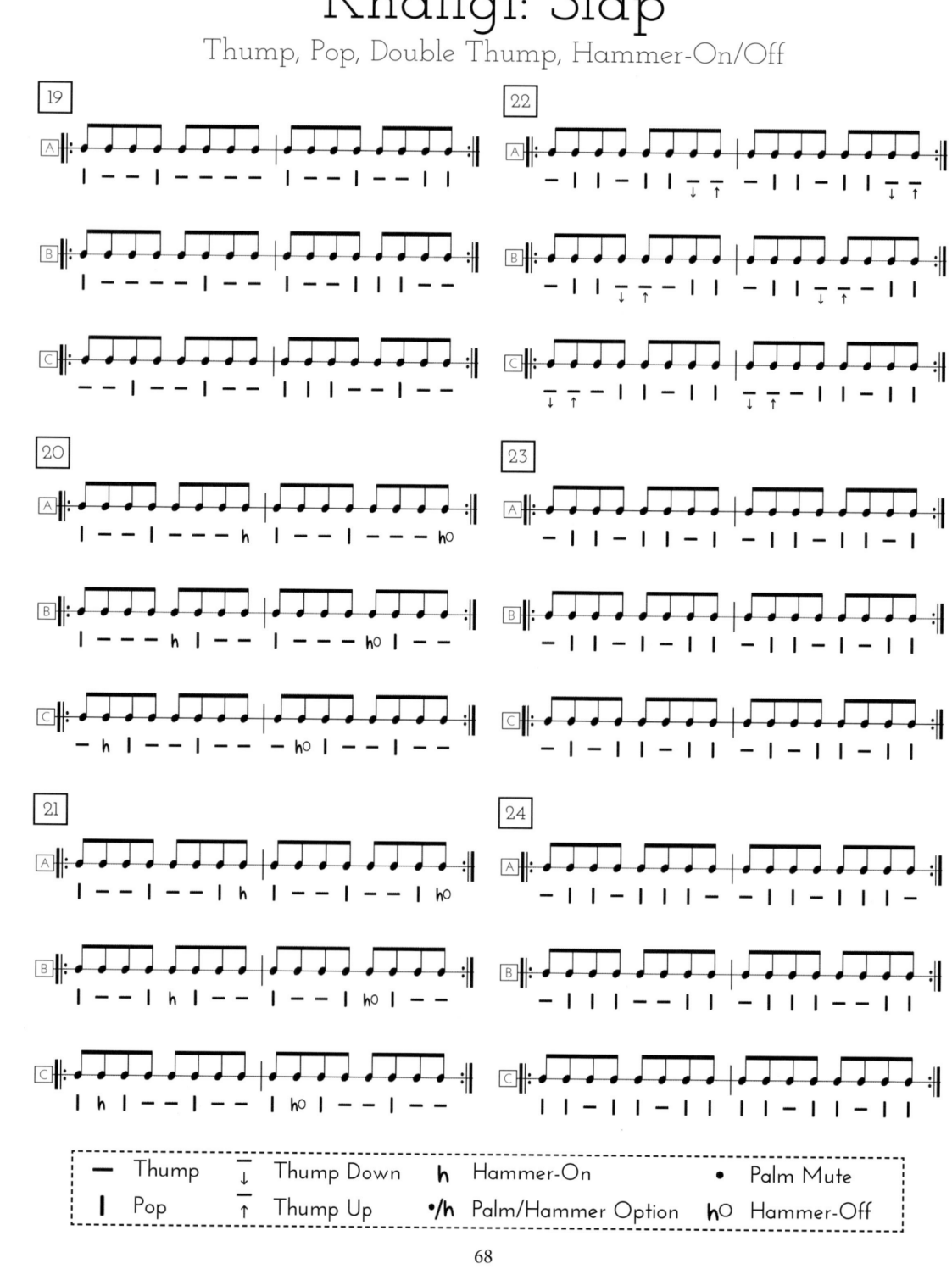

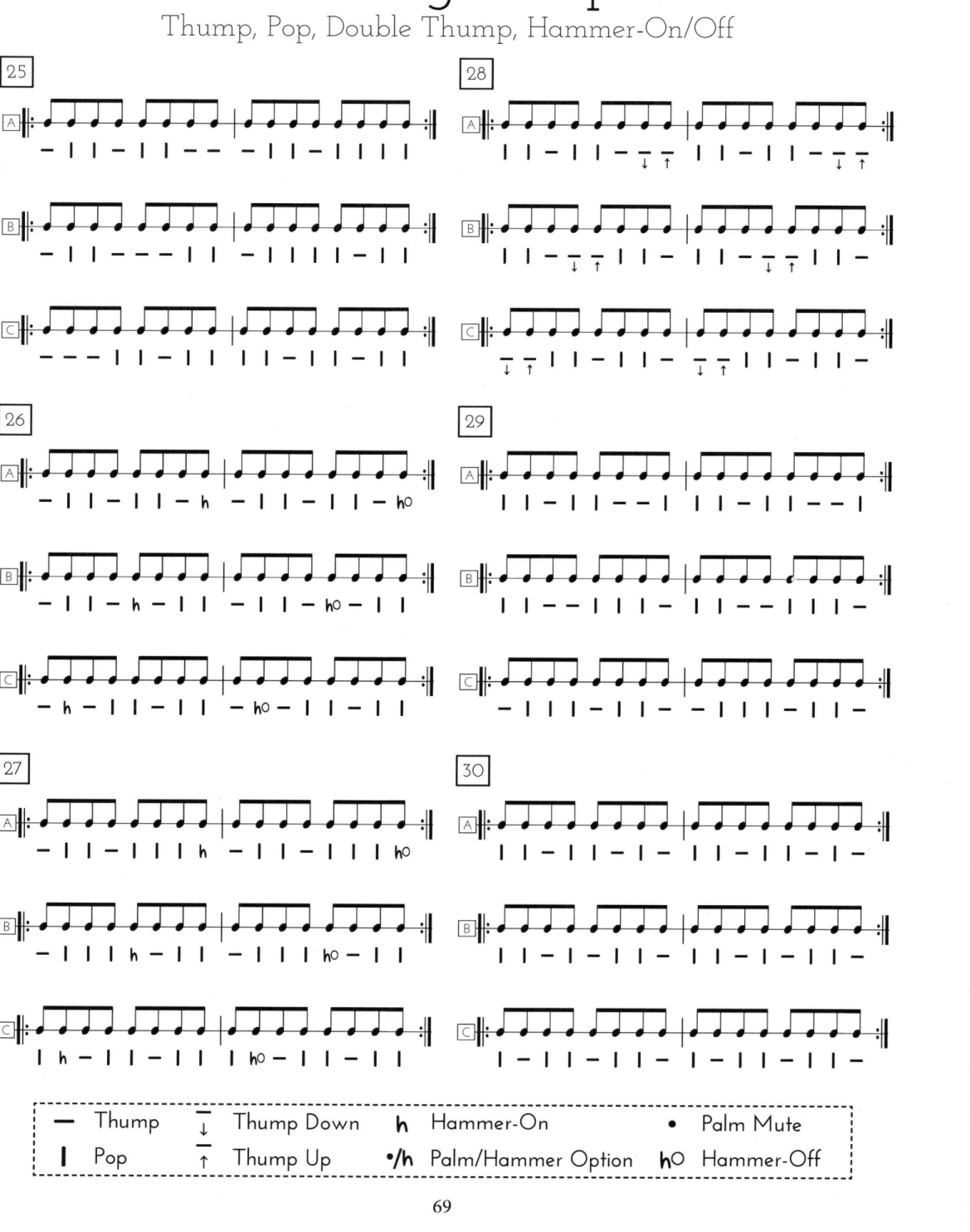

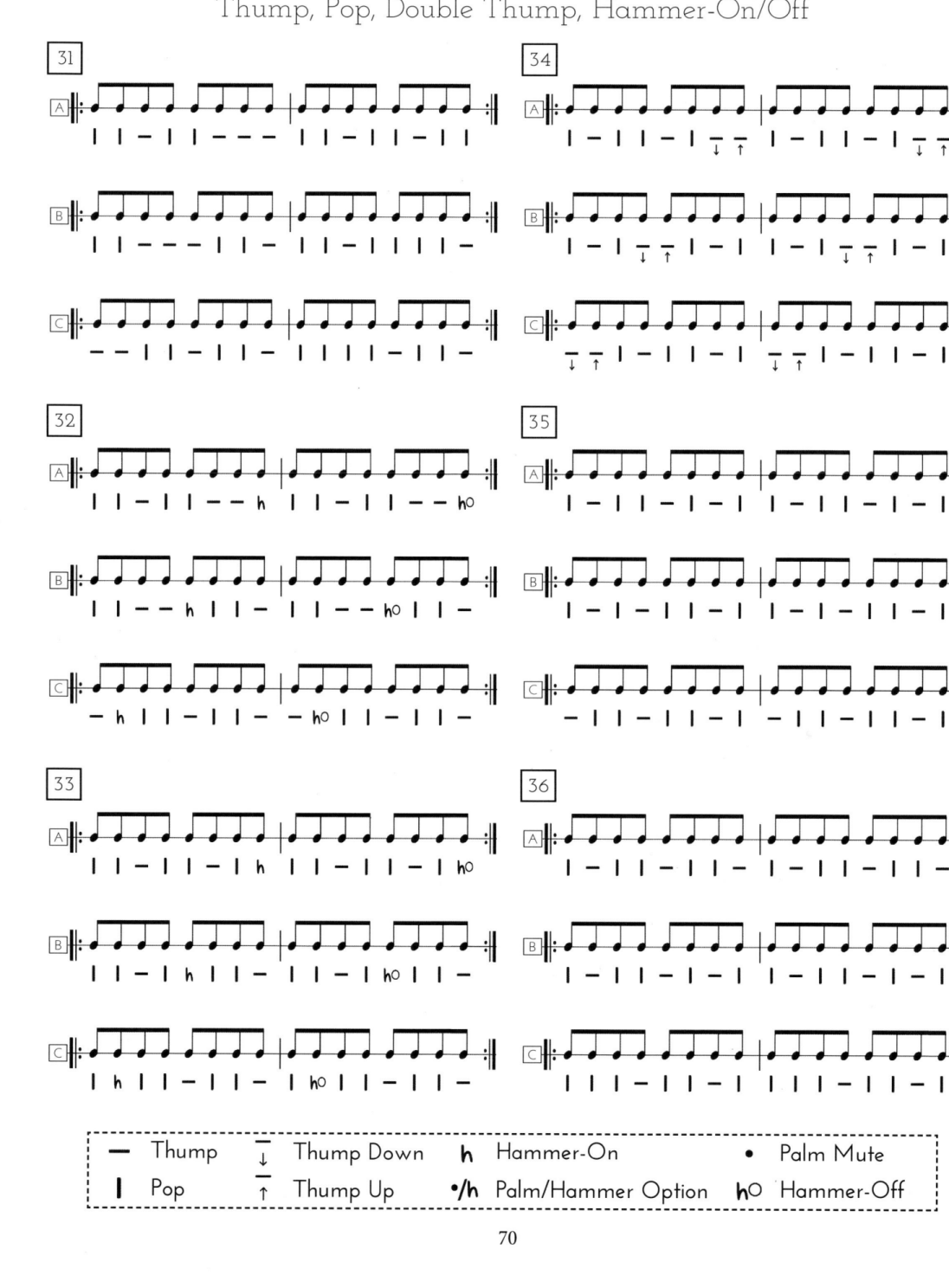

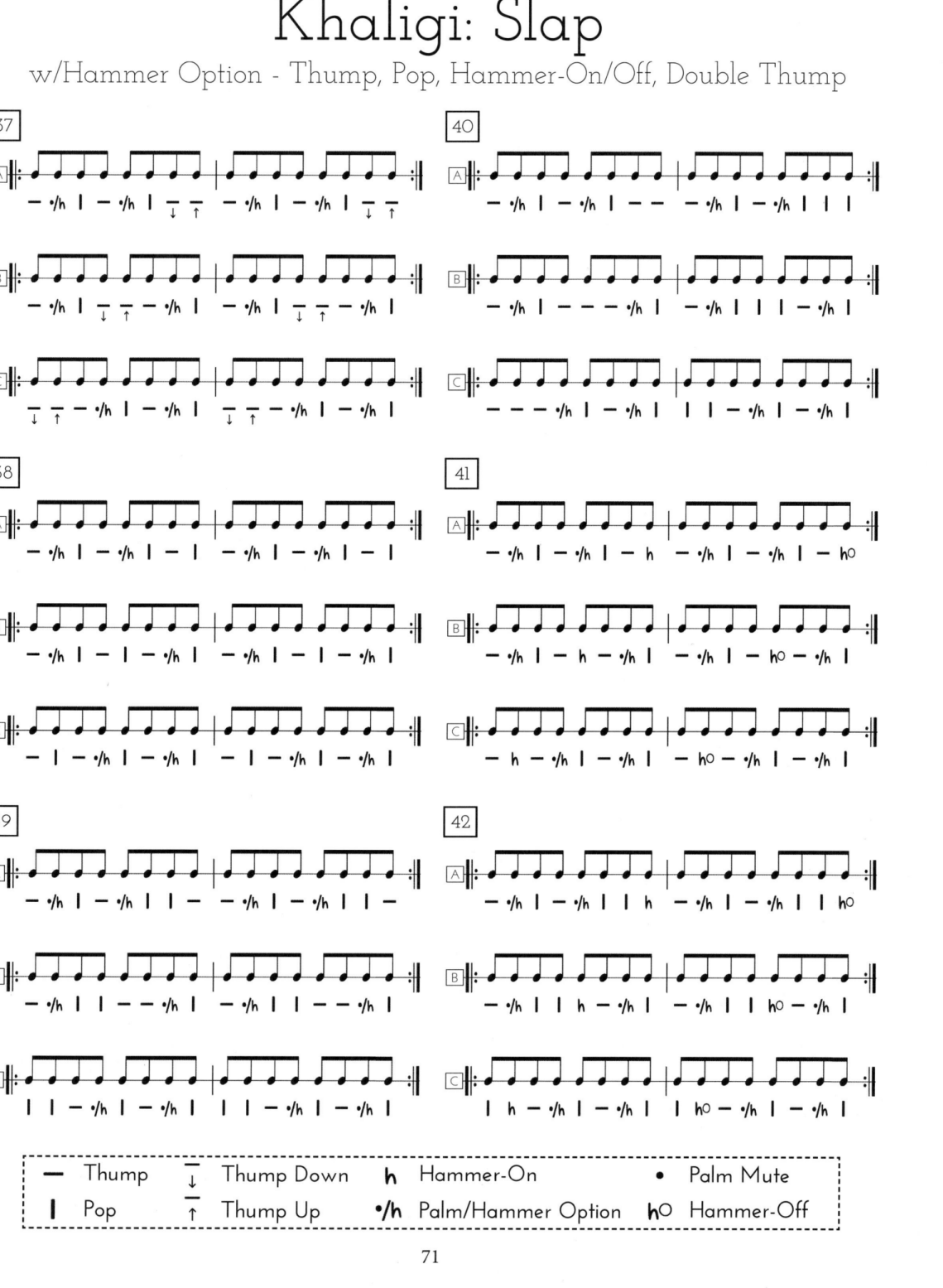

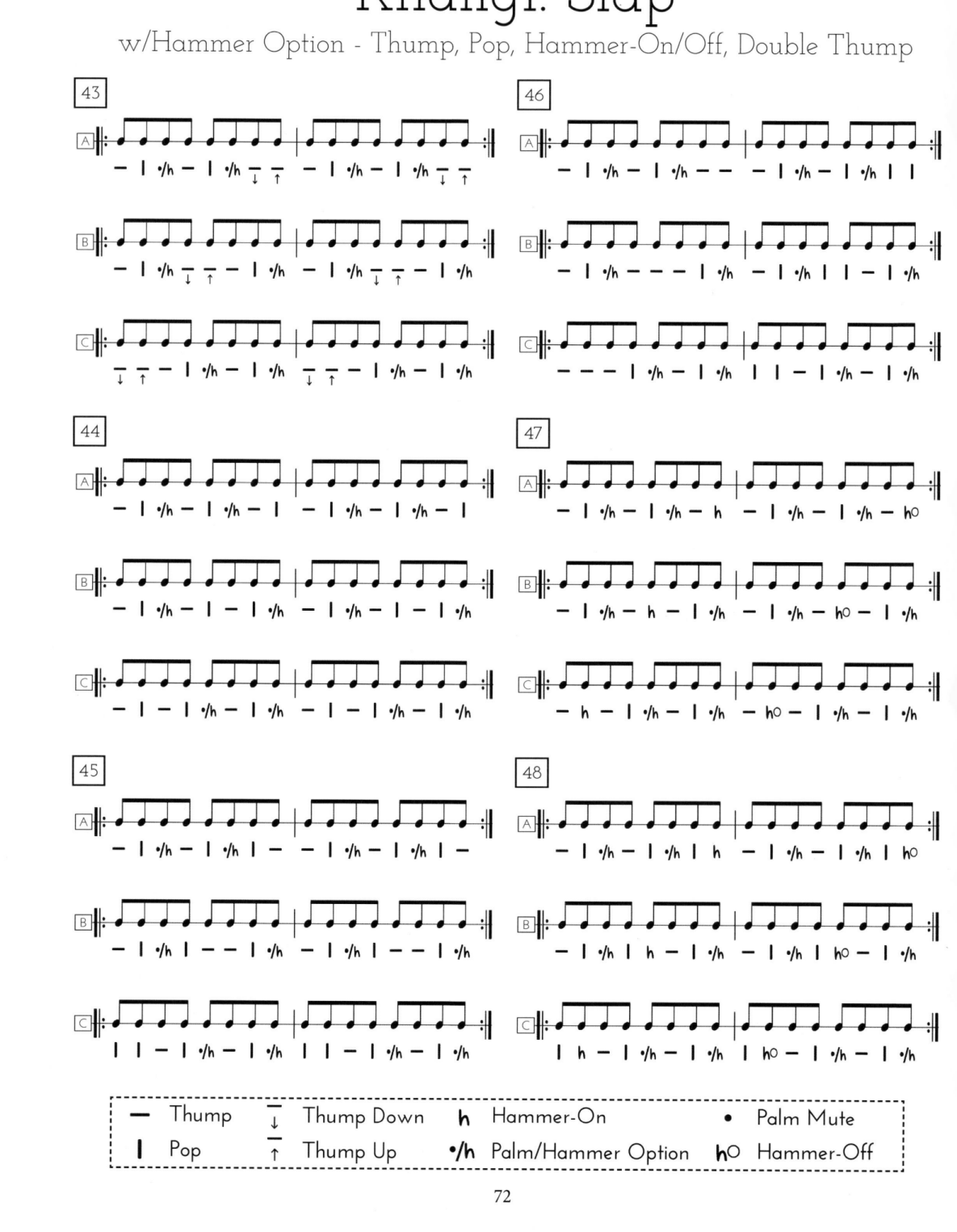

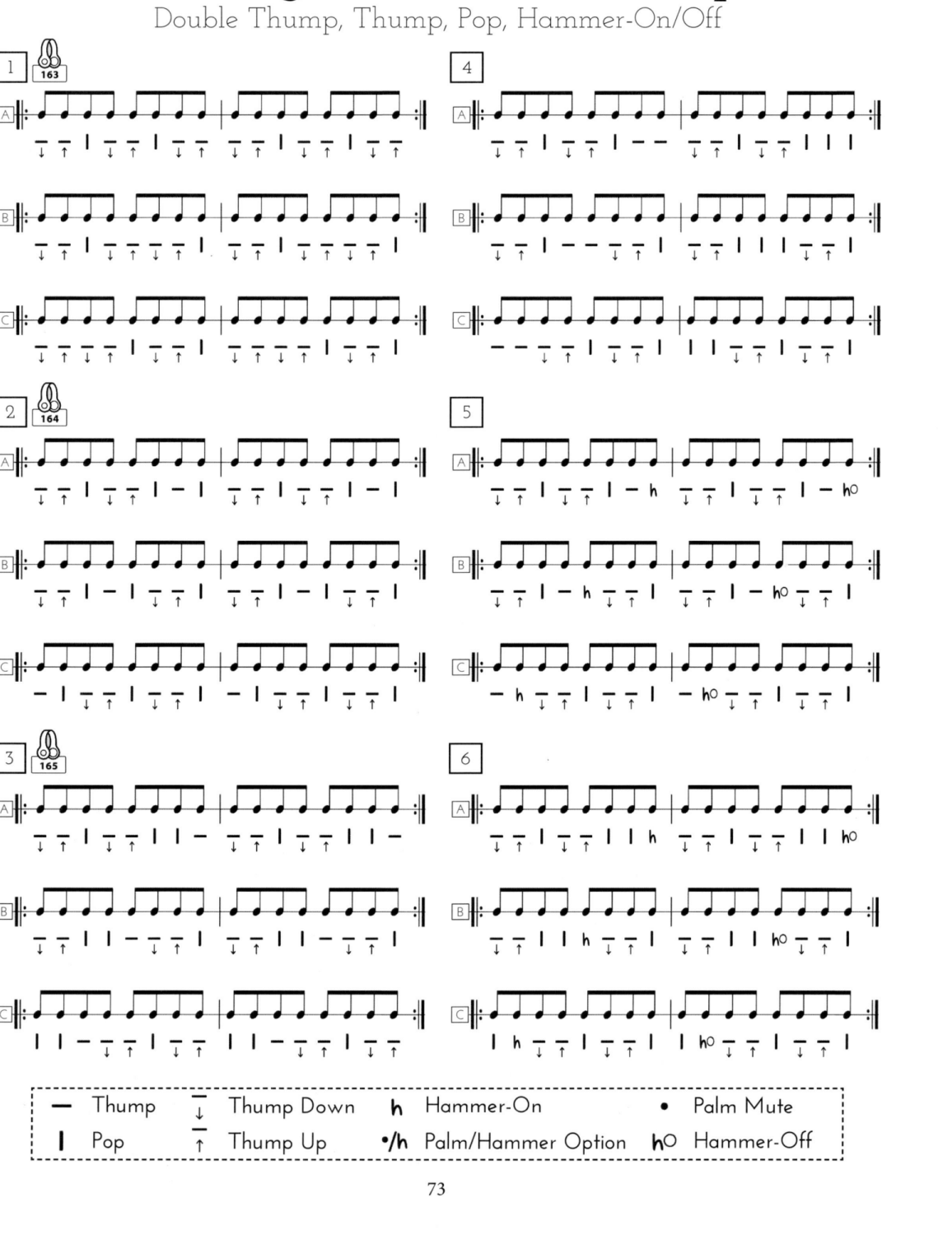

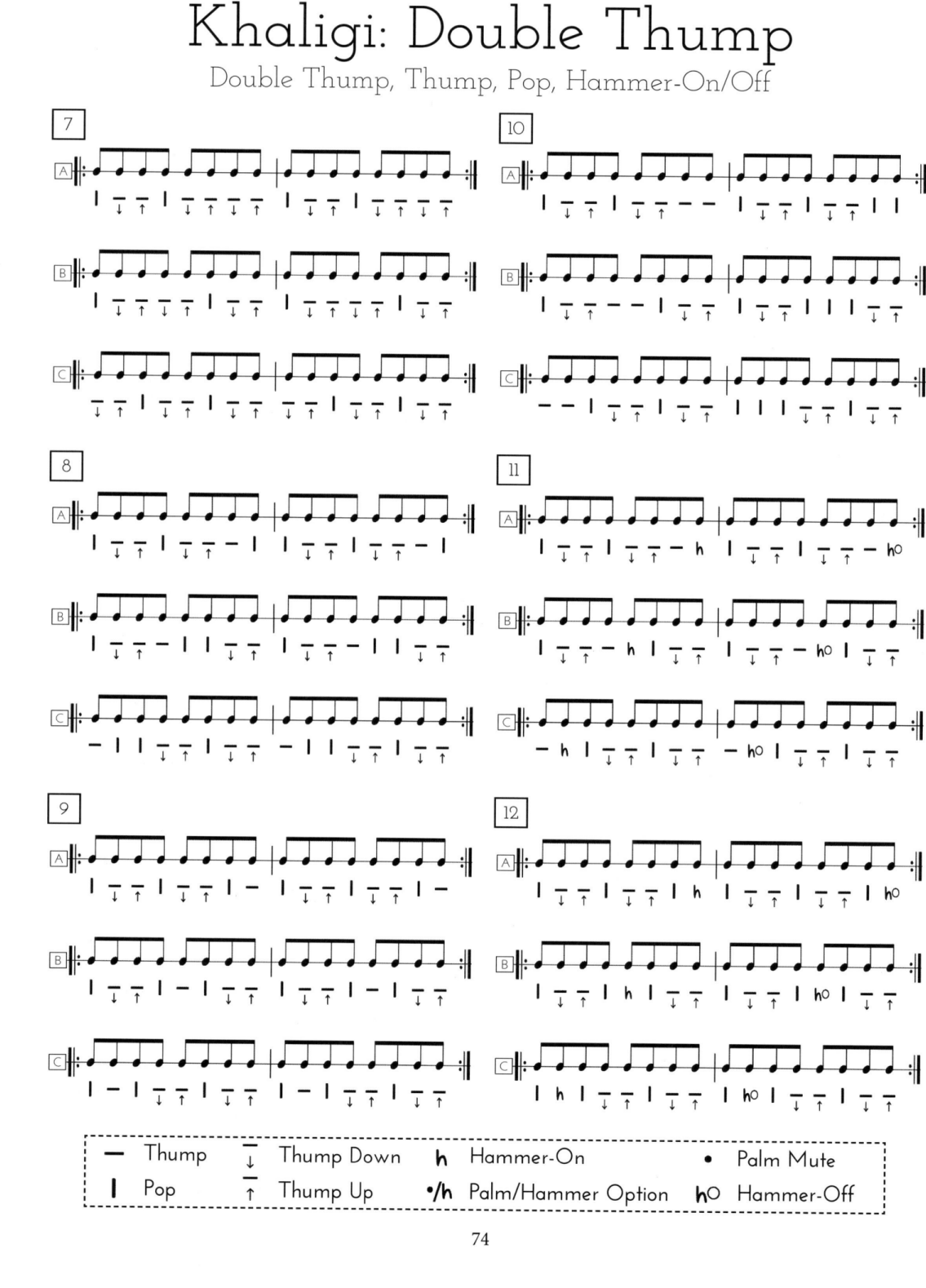

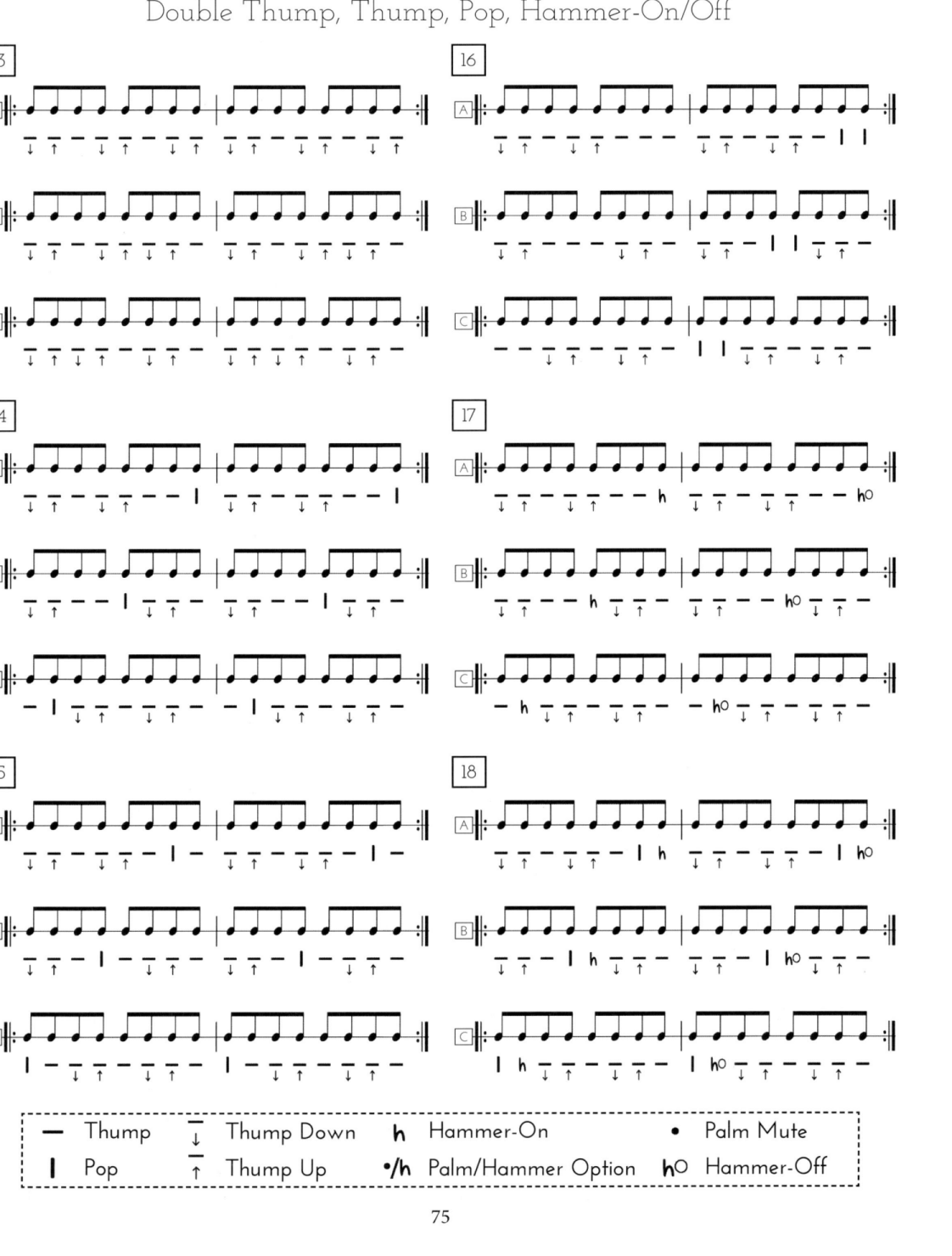

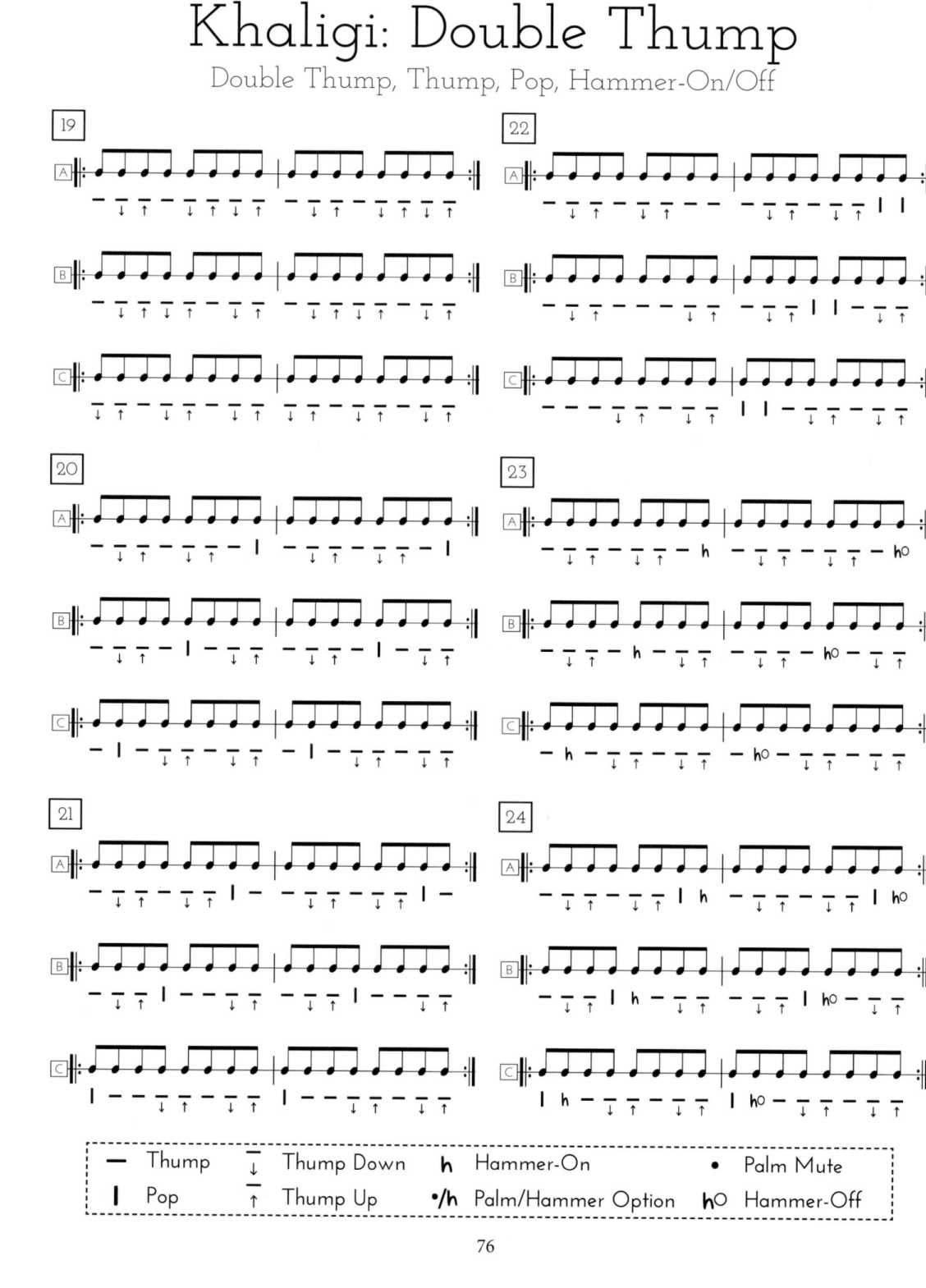

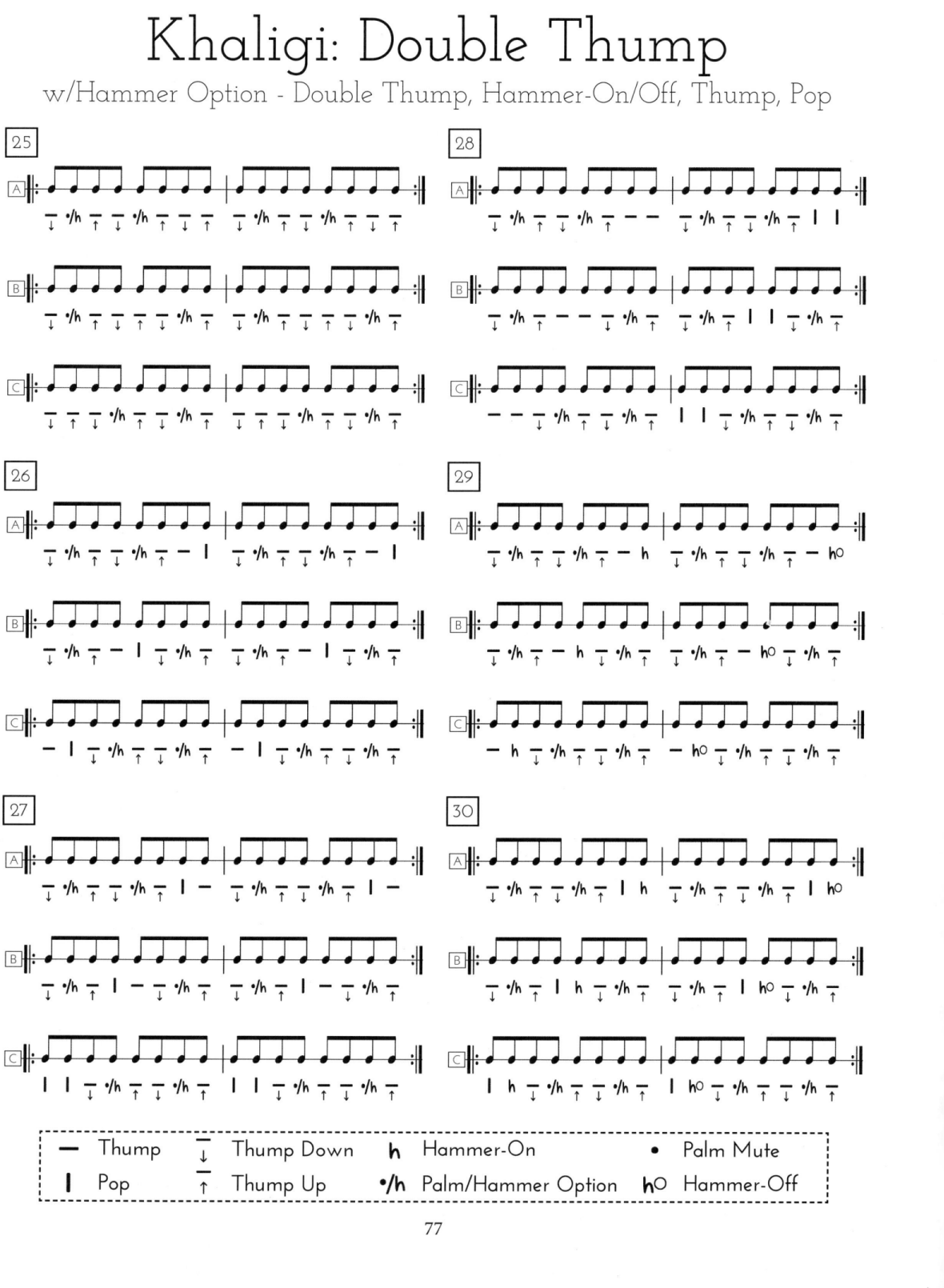

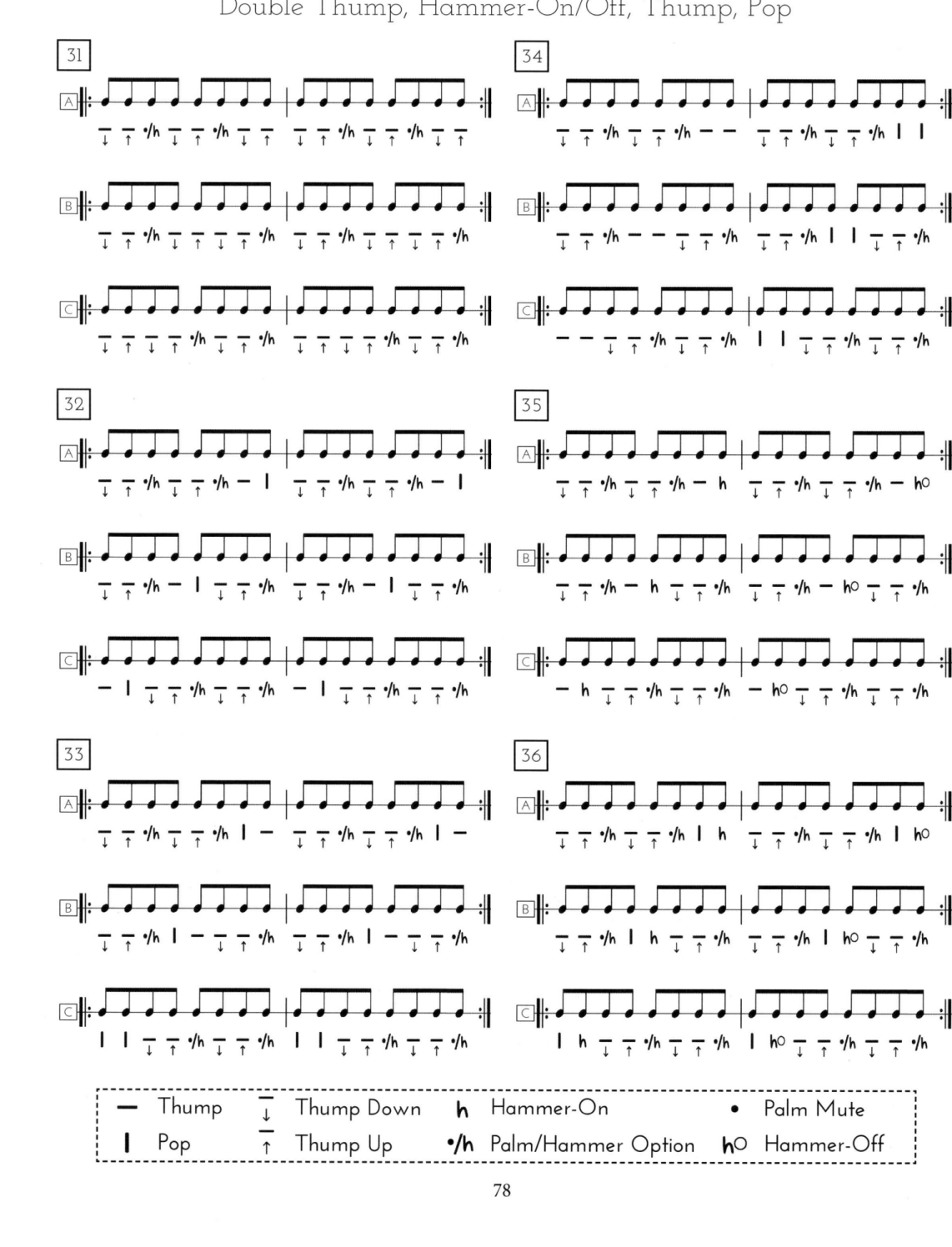

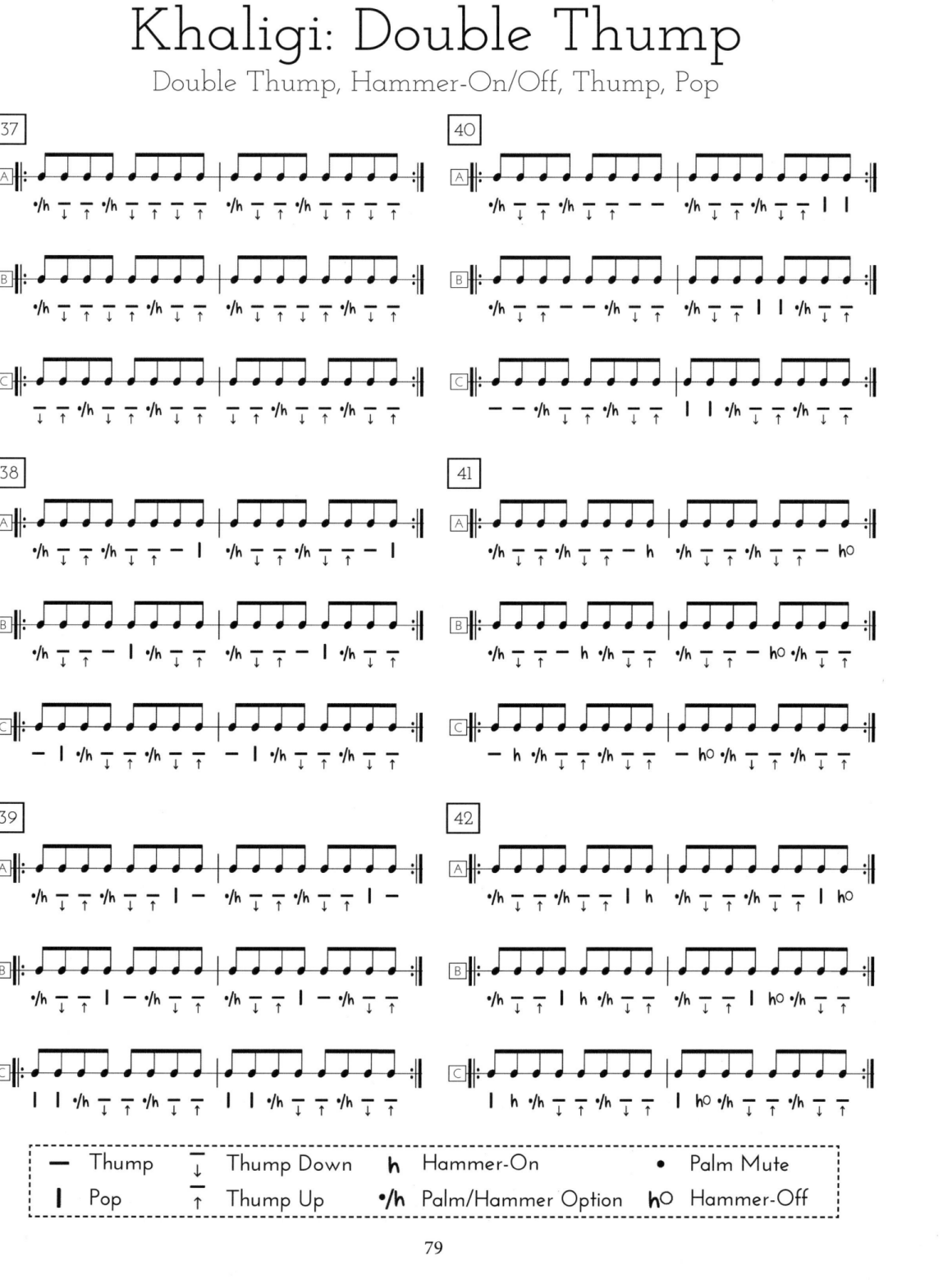

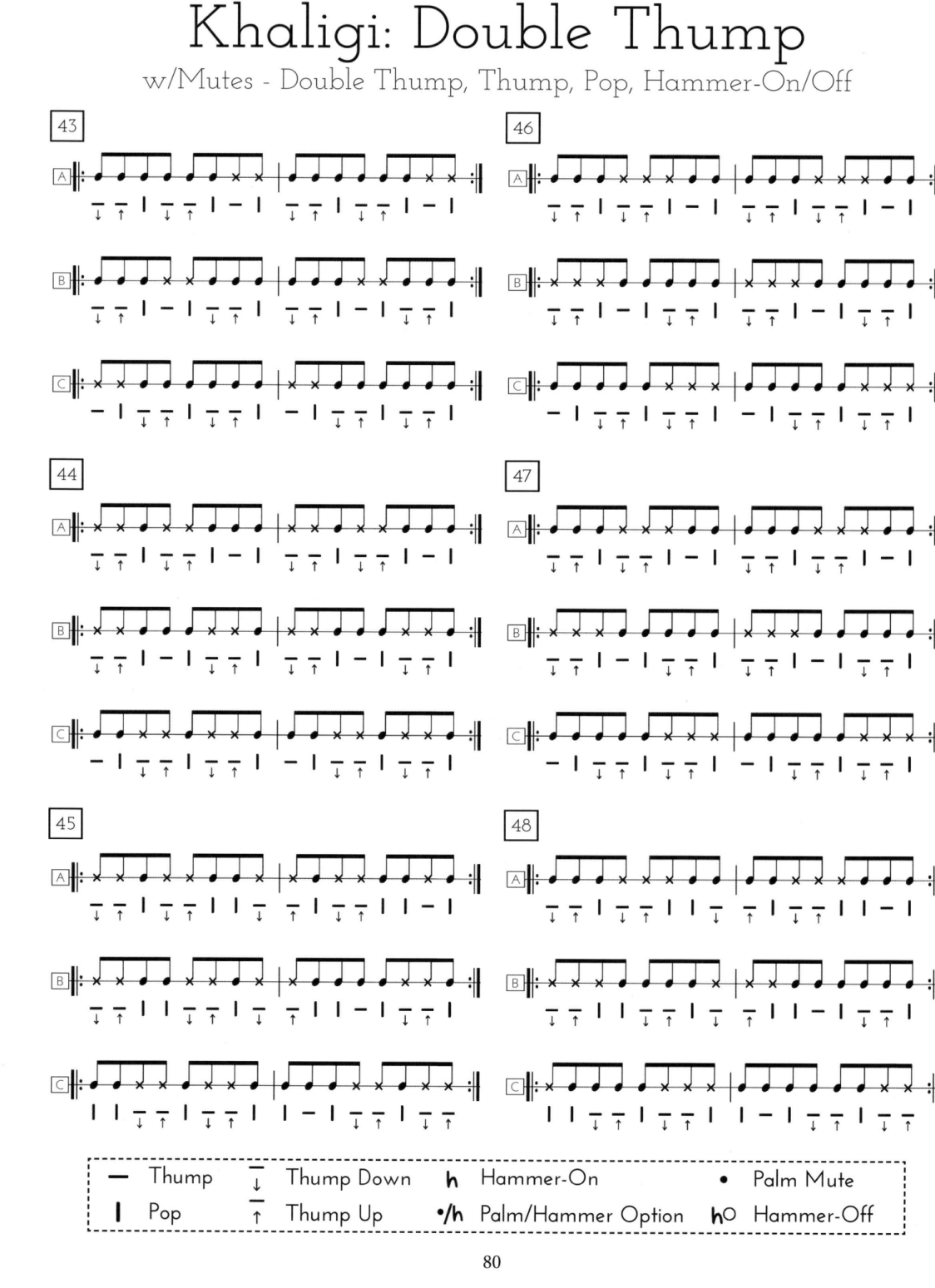

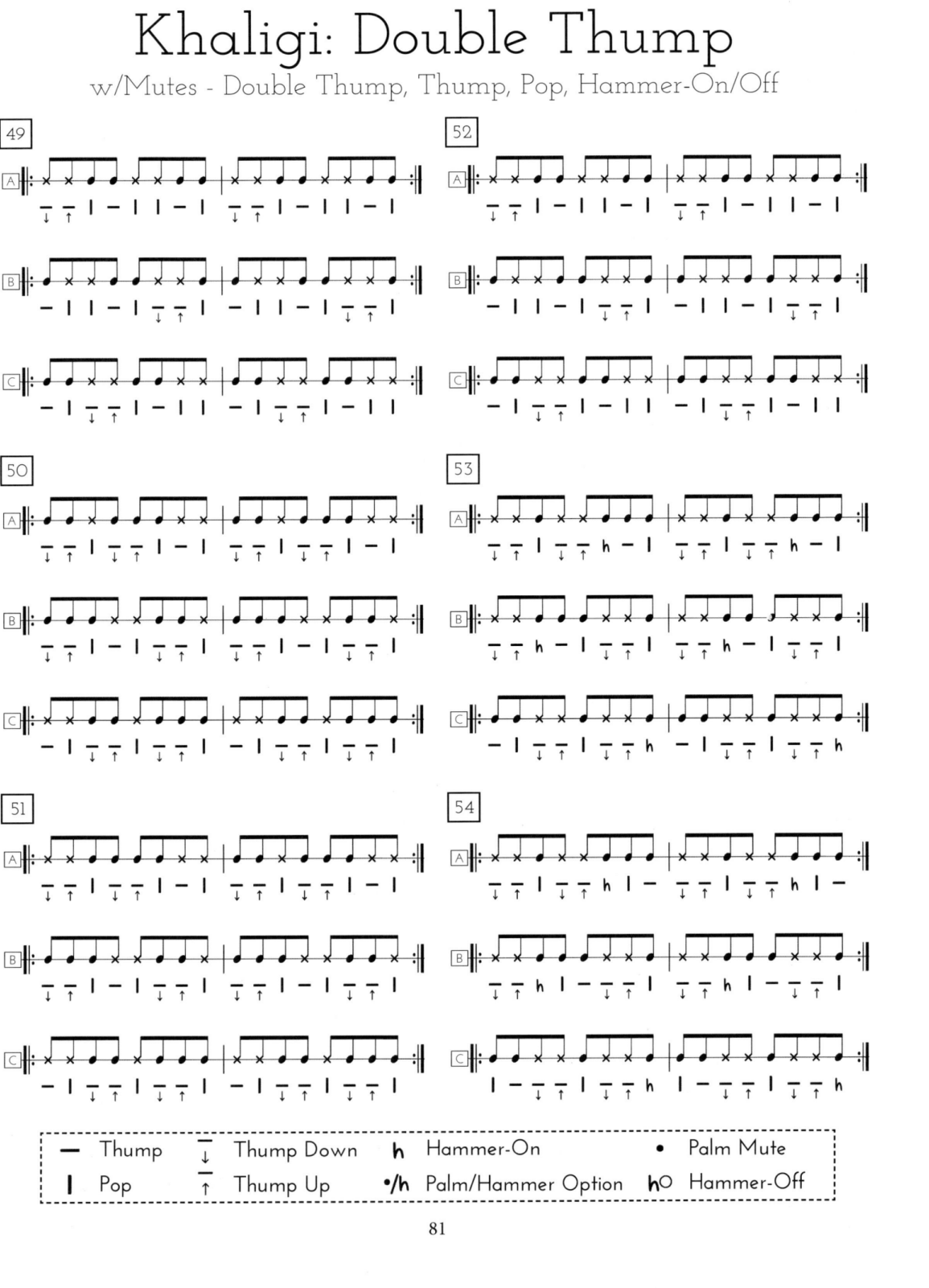

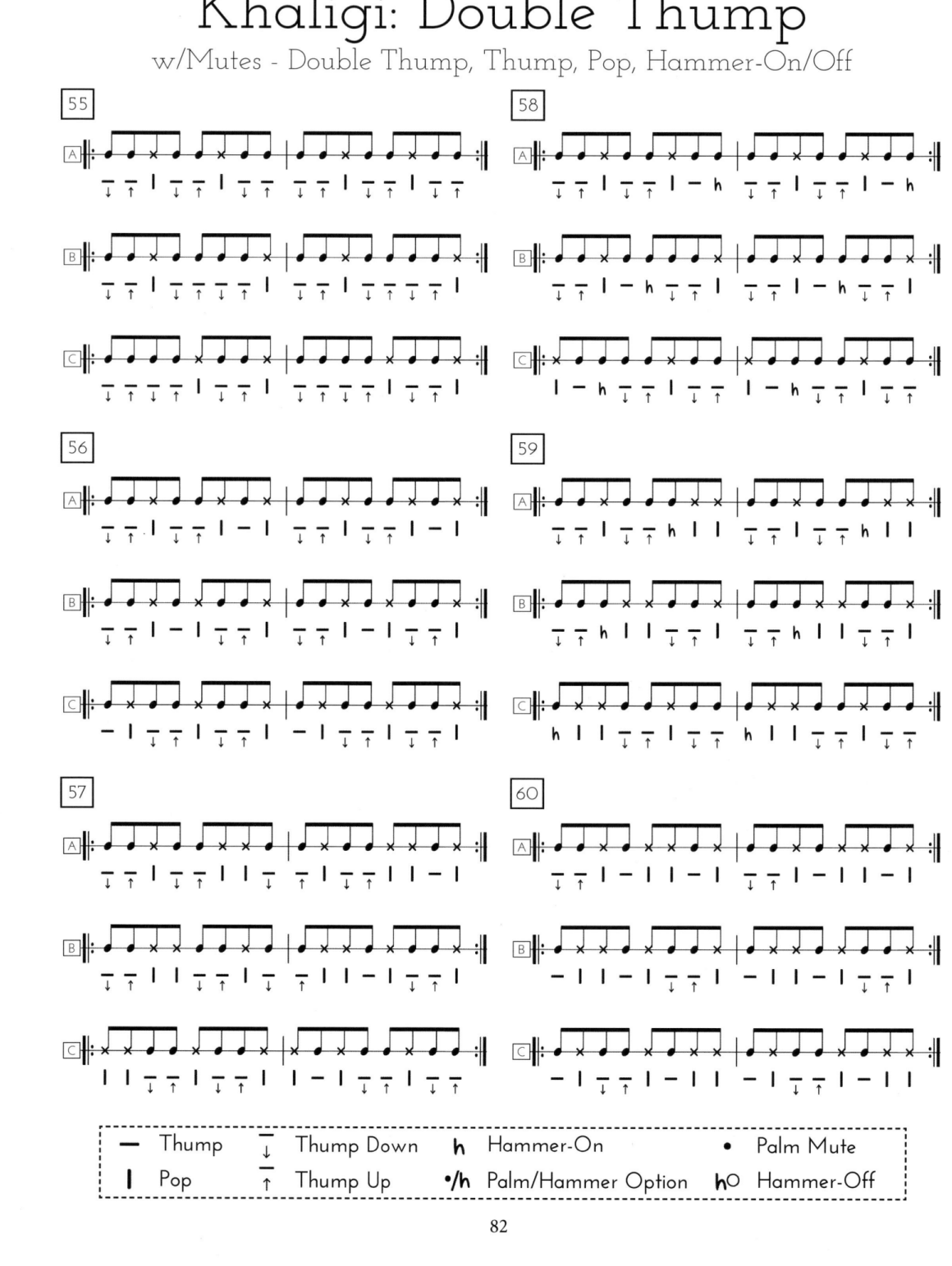

EXTRA PHRASES

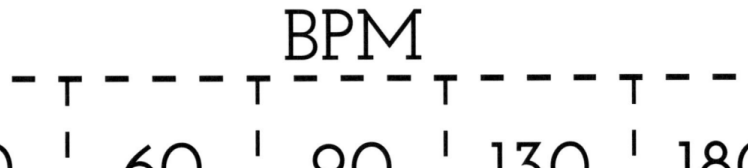

About This Section

The exercises in this section are extras. They contain every muted possibility for Groups of 2 and Groups of 3. Muted possibilities of Groups of 4 are not included simply because there are so many of them.

GROUPS OF 2

GROUPS OF 3

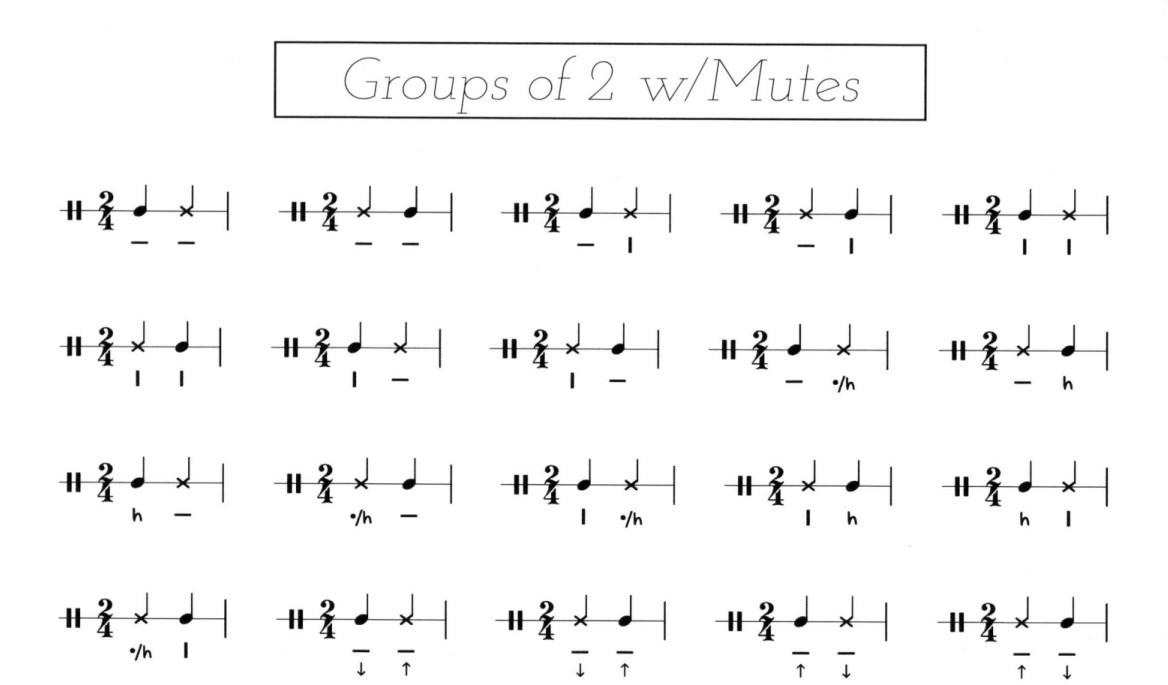

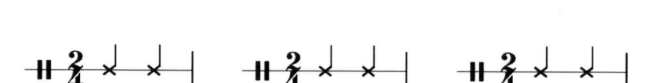

A - 3rd note is muted
B - 2nd note is muted
C - 1st note is muted
D - 2nd and 3rd notes are muted
E - 1st and 2nd notes are muted
F - 1st and 3rd notes are muted

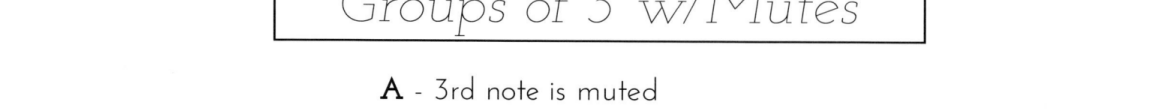

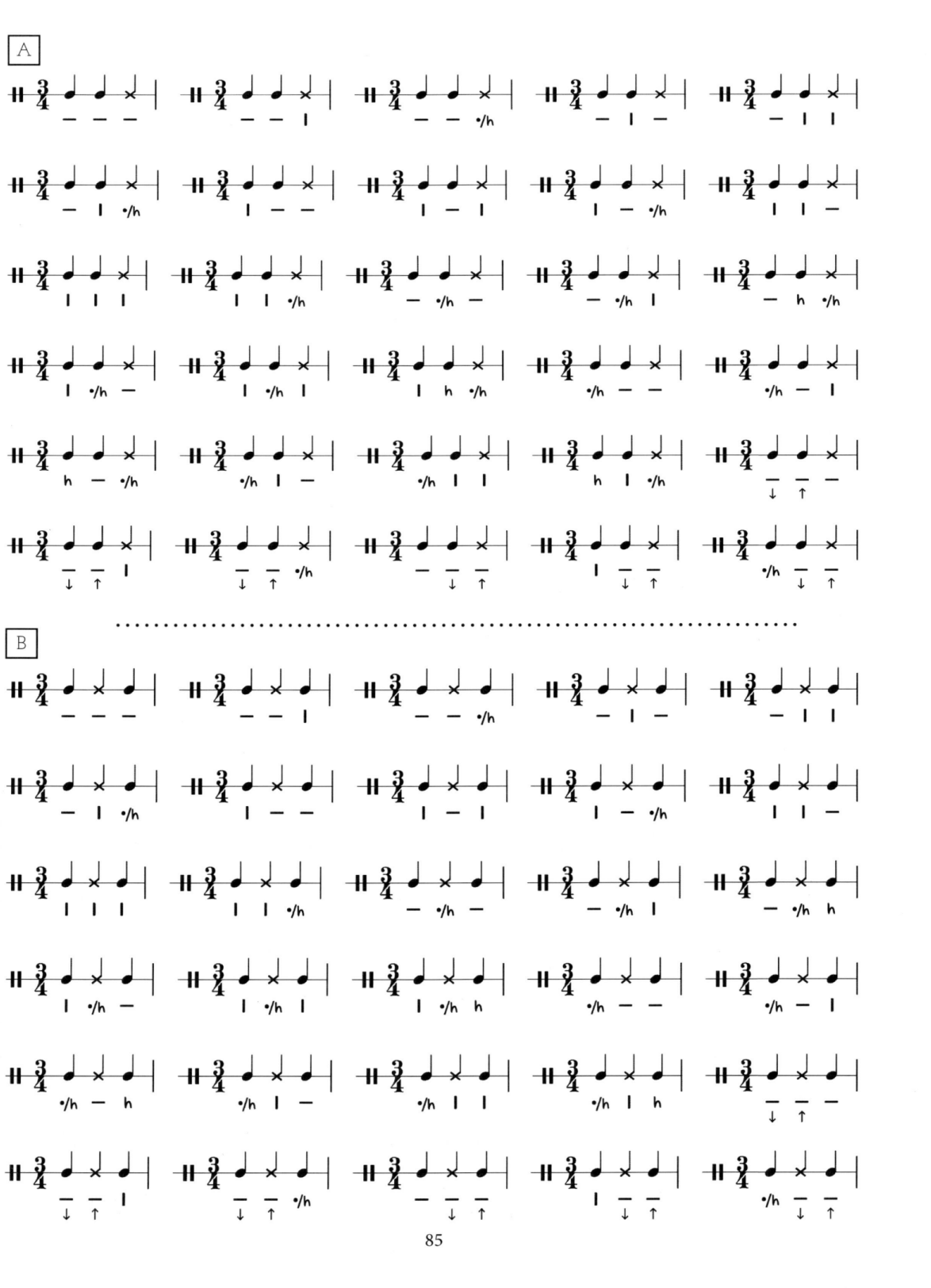

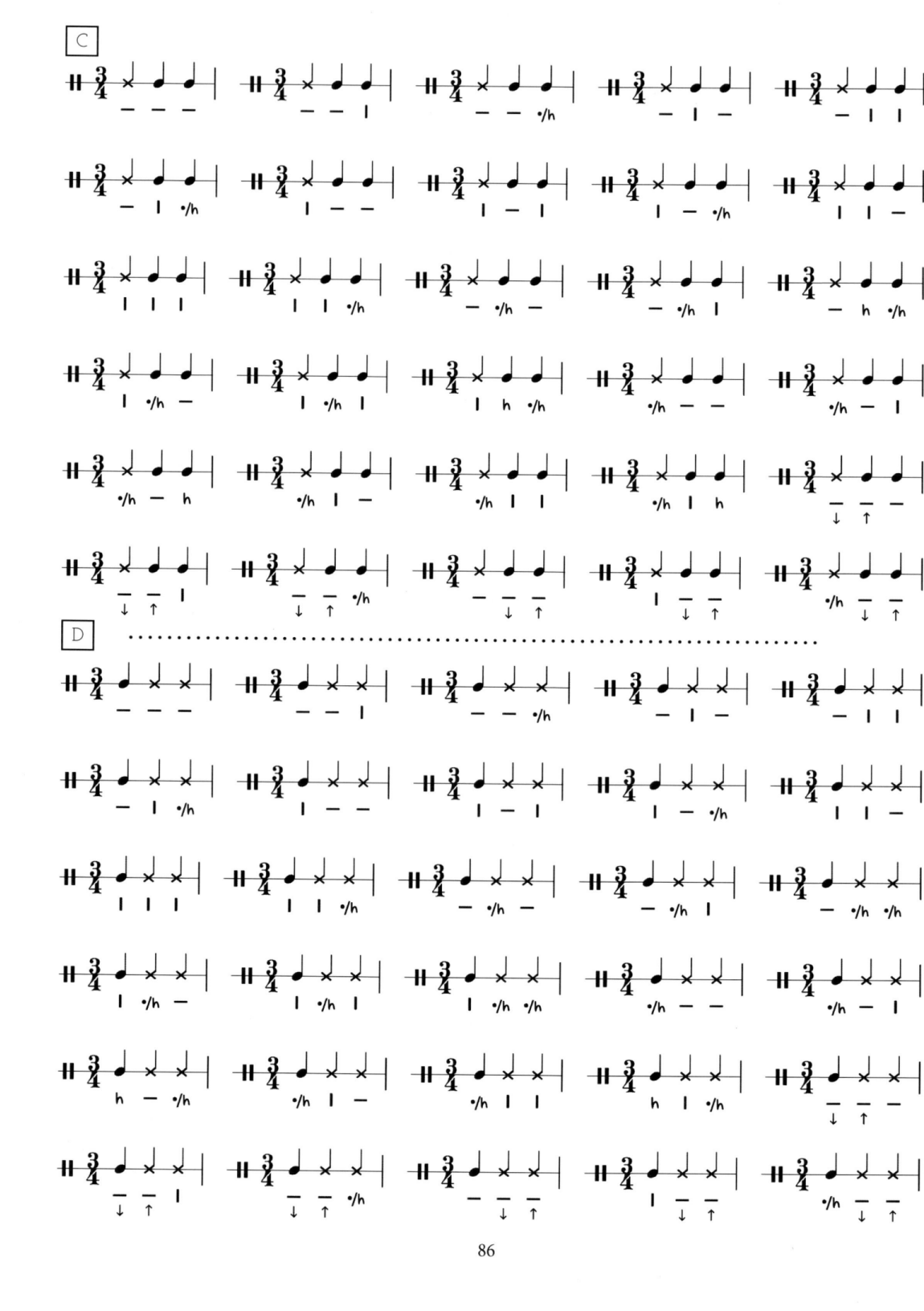

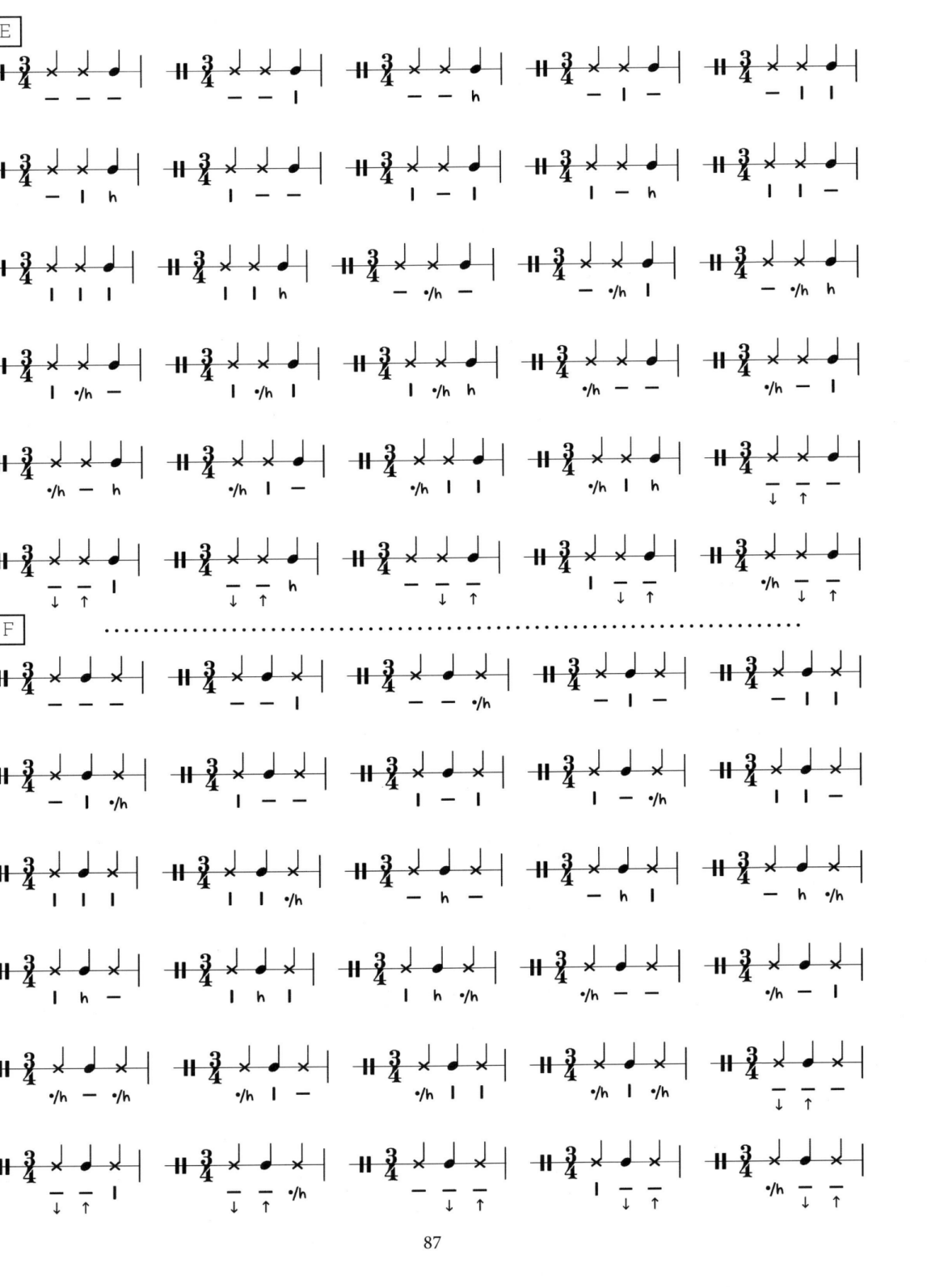

ABOUT THE AUTHOR

Josiah Garrett is a musician, producer, studio engineer, and teacher. Unsatisfied with traditional melodic and rhythmic pedagogy, Josiah has spent his years developing new and unique methods of describing, teaching, and understanding the fundamentals of music. These exercises, diagrams, and notation styles employ melody and rhythm as two sides of the same coin: a limitless forum of self-expression with practically infinite depth, and a discipline of rigorous study rooted in mathematics, periodicity, physics, and symmetry.

In addition to playing bass for 12 years, Josiah is a proficient multi-instrumentalist as well as a recording engineer and producer at Studio 1093 Boulevard in Athens, Georgia. This is Josiah's first published work and is focused around the bass guitar. "Slap Bass Encyclopedia" features a robust selection of technical practice and rhythmic exercises for slap and double thump style, and is an intense guide for the fellow curious bass player that wants to improve their slap bass performance.

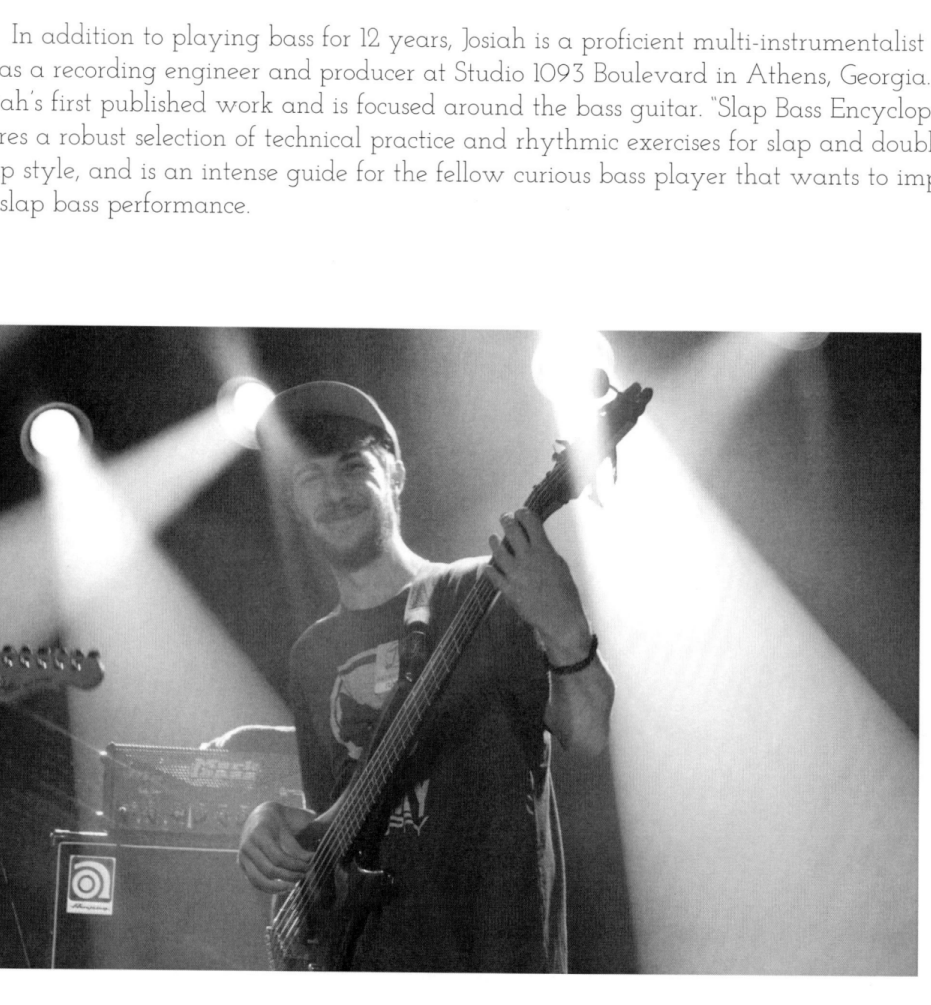

Letter from the Author:
The Bassist is a Member of the Rhythm Section

While melody, chords, harmony, pitch, and scales create "music" out of "sound", these sonic colors would drift into space without a rhythmic canvas upon which to paint them. Drum toms will resonate (pitch), and similarly a singer's voice is heard over time (meter). Even the snare drum needs to be tuned, just as reverb pedals have decay rate controls. Melody and rhythm are inseparable.

The bass guitar is a unique instrument: the bridge between the melodic world of guitar, piano, brass, and string instruments with the percussive world of drums. Only a few other instruments can claim a role in both the rhythmic and melodic voices of an ensemble (such as a bluegrass mandolin or lap-steel guitar, pitched percussive instruments like marimba or woodblocks, or a Hip-Hop DJ still spinning vinyl). The bass player is the backbone of the band. Your role, most importantly, is to be the glue that binds the other instruments together and the foundation upon which your band members will stand.

Notable slap players (Marcus Miller, Stanley Clarke, Victor Wooten, and Flea to name a few) have led successful careers on slap bass because they not only knew when and where to use slap style, but because they spent their careers developing the craft of being a better bass player first and a melodic voice in the mix second. Slap bass is a bright path upon which a rhythm player can venture into the limelight world of lead, but don't go too far down that road or you will lose sight of your roots as the commander of the low end.

THAT BEING SAID..... Slap Bass is one of the sexiest technical abilities in contemporary music, period. It defines the 70's and 80's era of funk and fusion, and is the product of a culture of musicians pushing past what had been thought possible on their instrument. Slap bass has a wide array of flexible tonal capabilities that are unique to the instrument. The timbre characteristics of a good slap bass player are immense and the sonic space it fills; massive. A slap bass player occupies all ends of the frequency spectrum and can create delicious grooves with the drummer. Slap and double thump techniques can be a loyal tool in your musical arsenal as a member of the rhythm section.

Because of the precise technique and dedicated practice required to execute slap bass, a high degree of discipline and dedication is essential. This book contains over 1,000 unique exercises for developing your style and technique in slap bass. Inspiration for these exercises is derived from drum rudiments and rhythms shared by professionals and educators around the world, and is designed to improve your technical abilities, precision and timing, rhythmic awareness, speed and accuracy, and dexterity for slap and double thump style.

When practicing these exercises, keep in mind where your "One" is: both where the rhythm begins and the downbeat of the measure. Bear in mind where you've been, where you are, and where you're headed within the exercise. To read and perform the exercises at tempo is recommended for nailing technical proficiency, but to fundamentally understand these rhythms means they must be memorized. If you make a mistake, do not play through it. If you do, you will encourage bad habits and poor technique. Take your time and remember: Fast is Last....

But most importantly, have fun!

-Josiah Garrett

Other Recommended Mel Bay Bass Books

Slap Bass Made Easy (Matheos)
Complete Blues Bass (Hiland)
Complete Funk Bass (Hiland)
Getting Into Slap Bass (Matheos)
Slap Bass for Five & Six-String Bass (Matheos)
100 Fretless Bass Workouts (Matheos)
50 Modal Slap Bass Workouts (Matheos)
100 R & B Soul Grooves for Bass (Matheos)
100 Rock & Roll Workouts for Bass (Matheos)
50 Two-Hand Tapping Workouts for Electric Bass (Matheos)
Bass Scales in Tablature (Betts)
Encyclopedia of Bass Arpeggios (Palermo)
Encyclopedia of Scales & Modes for Electric Bass (Roth)
Jazz Scales for Bass (C. Christiansen)
Learn to Burn: Electric Bass (Dozier)
Learn to Burn: 5-String Bass (Dozier)
Note Reading Studies for Bass (Evans)
Power Tools for 5-String Bass (Cockfield)
Rock Bass Technique (Hiland)
Scale Studies for Bass (Monoxelos)
Slappin' A Complete Study of Slap Technique for Bass (Ensign)
Walking Jazz Lines for Bass (Hungerford)
Comping Styles for Bass/Funk (Arnold)
Essential Blues Bass Grooves (DeRose/Barrett)
Percussive Slap Bass (Matheos)
Reggae Grooves for Electric Bass (Matheos)
101 Licks & Exercises for Bass (Gutt)
The Groove Book: A Study in Musical Styles for Bass (Ensign)
The New Sound of Funk Bass (des Pres)
The Ultimate Heavy Meta Bass Book (Matheos)
The Art of Solo Bass (Dimin)
Soloing for All Bass-Clef Instruments (Gately)
J. S. Bach for Bass (des Peres)
Essential Music Theory for Electric Bass (Garner)
The New Passion of Playing Bass (Washburne)

WWW.MELBAY.COM

WWW.MELBAY.COM